The Gift of Loss

Transforming Tragedy

Cathy Agasar

Deborah Kevin, Editor

HIGHLANDER
PRESS

Published by Highlander Press
501 W. University Pkwy, B2
Baltimore, MD 21210
www.highlander.press

ISBN 978-1-7343764-3-2

Printed in the United States of America.

Library of Congress Cataloging-in-Publication Data
Agasar, Cathy
The Gift of Loss/by Cathy Agasar
ISBN 978-1-7343764-3-2

Library of Congress Control Number: 2020934253

Managing Editor: Deborah Kevin
Editor: Kris Faatz
Cover Design: Kathie Jankauskas, KJanStudio LLC
Layout: Catherine Williams, Chapter One Book Production
Author Photo: Emory Graham, Ememories

Dedication

For all those who know the struggle is real...I pray you will find your path to self-care and live your best life every day. To Dave, Jennifer, Bryan, and Andrew...I love you grapes and bananas!

Contents

Foreword

I met Cathy at a women's networking group and felt naturally drawn to her because like attracts like. Cathy is a positive, glass half full kind of gal. I'm a positive, glass half full kind of gal. Cathy's faith sustains her. My faith sustains me. Cathy trusts that life is not free of difficulties, but we can make life more difficult by our reactions to them. Me too. And that's why we like each other.

The depth of our relationship changed one day, when my business partner at the time said, "Hey Denise, do you know Cathy, owner of Inner Spa. We had our first date." My business partner for over a decade, had gone through a challenging divorce, and we both often commented, and frankly prayed, that he would find a good, strong woman, "a believer" as us Christians are wont to say. When chance meets prayer, voila, a wonderful union occurs. Cathy and Jerry wasted no time, knowing they were perfect for each other and married shortly after that. I then really learned who Cathy was and is.

I simply had no idea of the depth of her difficulties. I had no idea that her husband was tragically killed, leaving her to raise three young children. I had no idea that her eldest son struggled(es) with the grips of addiction. While I knew Cathy owned Inner Spa, little did I know that she bought that business on little more than a wing and a prayer. I had no idea because Cathy was and is a glass half full kind of gal. I so love the line that I read once in a book by Byron

Katie, "Life doesn't happen to you. It happens for you. You don't have to like it. It's just easier if you do." That's Cathy. Cathy trusts all, and by all, I mean ALL that has happened to her has happened for her and not to her. Her faith is deep, way deep. Her faith is one I want to emulate. It does indeed sustain her. I'm beyond blessed to know her, to call her my friend. And after reading this book, I believe you'll feel exactly the same.

EnJOY,

Dr. Denise Chranowski
http://www.adosefromdrdenise.com

An Ordinary Day

For I know the plans I have for you, declares the Lord,
plans for welfare and not for evil, to give you a future and a hope.
Jeremiah 29:11

For Dave and me, that Thursday in August of 2006 started out much like any other humid summer day. We both rose early to get ready for a Chamber of Commerce meeting before work. At that time, I worked as vice president at a local bank, and Dave had a home office. He'd worked in my marketing consulting company since 2005, after leaving a long-held job in educational marketing and sales.

I dressed carefully for work in a sleeveless shirtdress, covering up my bare arms with a crisp navy jacket, choosing a floral scarf to match the dress, and tucking it under my jacket collar. Around my neck, I wore a simple gold cross necklace that Dave had given me twenty-two years earlier, the Christmas before we were married.

Our three kids—Jennifer, Bryan, and A.J.—enjoyed summer days spent lazing around and spending time with their friends. I'd add doing chores to that list, but couldn't honestly say they enjoyed them.

Our eldest, Jennifer, was fourteen that summer, a budding teen-ager full of life. She was organized and helpful when it came to family responsibilities and loved her younger brothers, but also enjoyed her time with her close circle of friends. She and her father had a very special relationship and could talk about anything, and often did. She was full of laughter and love, like me, in many ways.

Bryan, the middle child, was a lot like his dad. He was outgoing, funny, and not scared to try new things. He enjoyed sports and having his dad coach his baseball team; he also liked to do gymnastics and climb trees, which sometimes made my head spin. Like most 11-year-old boys, he could be stubborn and push the limits; I had recently begun to understand why someone at church had dubbed him "Cathy's challenge" when he was about three. He loved being a big brother because it was something his sister could never do.

Andrew Jacob, the youngest, was still learning his place in our little family. He loved his sister dearly and enjoyed spending time with her. He looked up to his big brother, and was always trying to do the same things; the boys had a love-hate relationship as only brothers can because they couldn't live with each other, but they couldn't live without each other either. A.J., as we began to call him (mostly because Andy, Drew, and Jake never really took), was a happy yet serious child who loved to watch Disney movies, swim, play video games, and be outside with his dad.

That day in August 2006, for the first time, Jennifer babysat her younger brothers for the couple of hours that Dave would be with me at the chamber meeting. The "what to do in an emergency" list hung on the refrigerator.

Because my office was in the opposite direction of our meeting, Dave and I both drove, leaving home one after the other. Our chamber was active, with an average attendance of over 120 people. Once a month, the chamber held a special program meeting that was always a "must attend" event because of its energy and positivity. That day, the program was a networking extravaganza, where each attendee got to meet and network with at least fifteen other business people.

After the meeting, Dave and I walked to our cars. I said, "Remember that the boys have haircut appointments this morning."

2

Then I remembered that I'd left some papers on the kitchen table. "Would you mind bringing those papers to me at the office later?"

"No problem," he said, kissed me, and drove off.

~

My day was going along swimmingly, very productive and creative. I was usually very focused at work, but that particular day it just seemed that I was especially on my game. I had spent the previous six months working on a web site redevelopment project that had zapped my creativity, so I felt good brainstorming marketing campaigns and getting plans finalized for a new marketing initiative. At that time, I was vice-president of marketing, working with a graphic designer, administrative assistant and my assistant manager.

I remember how positive and energetic I felt that day. My office was rather large, with a large window that filled the office with lots of natural light, and that morning especially, I loved how the light filled the space. I noticed the artwork on the off-white walls; I had hung a few of my own pictures but kept it conservative, and I'd also hung some of the marketing pieces I created for the bank.

About noon, my husband called to let me know he was downstairs by the back entrance to the office with the papers I needed. I took a break from my meeting with the rest of my team and went down to meet him. "Here are the papers you left at home," he said. He didn't get out of the car but handed me the papers through the open window.

I thanked him for bringing them over. "I'm sorry I forgot them, and you had to come up."

"No worries," he said. "I took the boys for their haircuts; Thim says hi. The boys both behaved themselves, and their hair looks good too." I smiled; it was good to hear Bryan and A.J. hadn't caused any trouble. Dave asked, "What should we have for dinner?"

It all seemed like such an ordinary conversation. "It's up to you and the kids," I said. "Surprise me."

He chuckled. "Ok."

"I love you," I said, and he said, "I love you too." Then I went back up to my office, and he drove out of the parking lot, heading home.

Crap! As soon as he was gone, I realized I'd forgotten to ask Dave about the kids' stuff for their trip the following week. They were going to visit my parents, and we had to be sure they had everything they'd need. With our busy schedules, we had to start planning now, buying any necessaries we didn't have yet, and deciding when the actual packing would happen. I picked up my cell phone and punched in Dave's number. Voice mail. "That's odd," I thought. He always answered his phone when he was at home with the kids.

Even as I set my phone back down, sirens split the silence. I heard them as clearly as if I'd been outside. I said a prayer for those receiving medical attention and hoped Dave had gotten home safe. Surely he had, I thought. But a nagging feeling kept lingering. I called Dave's cell phone again, but still no answer, so I hung up without leaving another message. I went back to the marketing materials on my desk, telling myself Dave was probably fine, just busy with work at home.

My assistant manager and I had just about finished our brainstorming session when the phone on my desk rang. I saw the caller ID: St. Mary Medical. Not giving it a second thought, I answered with professionalism and a smile.

"Good afternoon, this is Cathy."

"Hi Cathy, this is Heather at St. Mary Hospital. I don't know if you remember me or not, but we sat together at the hospital's fundraiser back in May." It only took me a second to put a face with the name as Dave and I had enjoyed talking with her at the event.

"Hi, Heather. I do remember you. It was so nice to meet you and spend that evening with you and your husband," I said. "How can I help you today?"

"Cathy," she said, "there's been an accident, and I need you to come to the hospital. Do you have someone who can drive you here?"

"An accident?" I didn't understand. I didn't think the word *accident* could mean anything to me personally. "Who?" I asked. "What's happened? I can drive myself," I added, hearing how calm my own voice sounded.

"Cathy," Heather said gently, "Dave was in an accident. Everything will be explained when you get here. I need you to have someone drive you, though. Is there someone with you that can do that?"

It still didn't seem real. Dave. An accident. Someone to drive me, as if I couldn't do it myself. Why couldn't I? "Okay," I told her. I clung to what I knew, getting things done in my usual competent, professional way. "I can do that," I said. "I'm about five minutes away. Where do I need to go?"

"Come to the emergency room, and they will direct you," she said.

"Okay. I'll be on my way in just a couple of minutes." Still, my own voice sounded amazingly calm in my ears. "Thanks, Heather," I added as if she were a client touching base. And with that, I hung up the phone.

The Upside Down

~

Don't be afraid, for I am with you.
Don't be discouraged, for I am your God.
I will strengthen you and help you.
I will hold you up in my victorious right hand.
Isaiah 41:10

My mind was racing yet calm; it was a weird feeling. My assistant manager, Kirk, was still in the room with me, looking at me with a question in his face. I told him I needed him to drive me to the hospital; we could take my car. He agreed at once.

Then I went to the operations director, because my boss was out of town, and told him that I needed to leave because my husband had been in an accident. I asked if he could please find out what had happened as they would not tell me anything on the phone. By then, I was starting to lose it a little. Because the operations director did a lot of work with the township, somehow, at that moment, I thought he could find out what was happening and make it better.

My heart was racing, and my mind kept going in circles as I tried to understand what had happened. Did my phone call distract Dave and cause the accident? How long would he be in the hospital? What would his recovery look like? What kind of care would he need? Kirk and I got into the car and pulled out of the parking lot, but there was a police barricade right out in the street. The police made us turn around and go a different way. Any other time that would have annoyed me, but that day I simply gave Kirk directions as he was not familiar with the area to make the detour. I am still thankful to this day that I could not see beyond the barricade.

As Kirk drove, I was on my phone, making calls to ask for prayer. My first call was to my mother in Illinois.

She answered the phone quietly. "I'm in a meeting, can I call you back?"

I said, "Yes, but please pray for Dave. He's been in an accident. I'm headed to the hospital now."

She agreed and told me to keep her posted before we hung up. I dialed the phone again, this time to my dear friend and associate pastor Alicia; the call went to voice mail. *Beep.* "Alicia, it's Cathy. Please call me. Dave's been in an accident, and I need you to meet me at the hospital. Thanks."

I needed someone to talk to, right then. My heart was racing crazily, and I was having trouble catching my breath. I called Joe, Alicia's husband, and was relieved when he answered.

"Hello," he said.

"Joe," I blurted out, "Dave's been in an accident, and he's at St Mary's. I tried to call Alicia, but she didn't answer. Can you please call her and ask her to meet me at the hospital?"

I spoke so fast, and hysterically, he could barely understand me. "Cathy, calm down," he said. "What happened?"

"I don't know; they wouldn't tell me anything, just that I needed someone to drive me to the hospital." My professional veneer was gone, and I thought I might burst into tears at any second. "Can you please pray, and try to reach Alicia?" I begged.

"Yes, I'll do both," Joe said. His calmness steadied me. As we hung up, my phone rang; it was Alicia. I answered the phone, and I told her what I knew. "Please, can you meet me at the hospital? I don't know what's going on, and I don't know who's with the kids. I need someone with the kids."

"I'll make a call," she said, promising to meet me as quickly as possible.

My next call was to another friend at the chamber who we had just seen that morning. I am not sure why I called her, but as I told her what was happening, I again babbled about the kids being home alone; she said she would leave to be with them. I felt a little more settled, but that feeling was only temporary as we pulled up to the emergency entrance at the hospital.

As we pulled up to the emergency room entrance, and I got out of the car and entered the building. My body felt like it belonged to someone else as I pushed myself to walk through the doors. Heather, bless her heart, was there to meet me. (I later learned that she wanted to be there so I would have a friendly face as the events of that day unfolded.) She held my hand and walked me down a hallway. We went into a room that was separated from the waiting area, which was filled with people.

The two of us sat in the small room. Heather told me the doctor would be in shortly to talk with me. Kirk soon came in and joined us too.

Sitting in that room seemed like an eternity. I don't know exactly how long it was, but Heather did leave at one point to find out where the doctor was. In my heightened state of anxiety, I did the only thing I could do; I picked up my phone again and began making calls. I felt like I desperately needed a lifeline to the outside world: I couldn't just sit here in this silence, not knowing anything. My first call was back to the operations director at work. I told him I was at the hospital, but they were not telling me anything, and I begged and pleaded for him to call the township and find out what he could. My next call was to another dear friend, Bill, who worked at another bank. I asked, "Will you please pray for Dave and me?"

"Oh," he said, "I heard all the sirens and prayed everyone would be okay," and then he did the most selfless thing and said, "I'll be right over."

~

True to his word, Bill showed up a few minutes later and sat with me. I had called the operations director at work yet again, but he had nothing he could tell me other than that it was a bad accident. (Much later, I learned he had found out more details about the accident, but could not bring himself to tell me about them over the phone.) By this point, I was growing more and more anxious.

The doctor finally came in, and I looked at him without really seeing him; to this day, I cannot remember what he looked like or even his name.

"I'm sorry," he said. "Your husband's injuries were extensive. There was nothing more we could do." He told me that Dave had been revived at the scene and again in the hospital, but they were unable to revive him a third time.

Nothing more they could do. I refused to accept it or even under-stand it. I screamed, "You have to try again."

Bill simply hugged me. That's when Alicia, my associate pastor, entered the room.

She took over. We cried and hugged as though my life depended on it; I actually think it did for those first moments. I remember the doctor saying that I should sit down and take as much time as I needed, and offered to call anyone I needed him to. He said some-thing else, but I couldn't hear it or don't remember what it was.

Without even realizing what I was doing, I picked up my phone and called my mother. She answered immediately and asked how Dave was.

My voice sounded flat and dead, as I answered. "He's gone."

"What?? What happened?"

I don't remember what I told her. I do remember when she said, "We'll be on the road as fast as we can. I'll call your dad, and we'll see you soon." My parents live in central Illinois, so driving to Pennsylvania takes about 14 hours; I had no idea what *soon* meant at that moment, but I was comforted knowing my mother was coming.

As I sat there in shock, I realized there were more people in that little room (which I later learned is called the "crying room"). One of them was the president of the hospital, who came to see if he could lend any support. We knew each other through the chamber as well as through the bank where I worked. Then the senior vice president of my bank, along with a fellow vice president and friend, showed up to offer support. I was so thankful to all of them for being there because I could not function and had no idea what to do next.

Liz, the senior vice president at the bank, took charge of the situation and found out what needed to be done. She told me, her voice soft, "Cathy, you need to make a few decisions quickly regarding his body."

What? How was I supposed to make those decisions? I had no idea what he would have wanted me to do. I'd never thought anything like this could happen. *Think.* I tried to remember anything he had ever said about it, but all I could remember, hopelessly and helplessly, was that we'd planned to draw up our wills the following week when the kids were away at their grandparents'.

Liz interrupted my spiraling thoughts. "Cathy," she said quietly, "you can take time, but keep in mind they have to know soon to successfully harvest tissues."

Harvest. That word snapped me awake. I still don't know whether I consciously made the decision that my husband's tissues should be donated, or whether I was just reacting to the need to make a decision, but I said they should do it. That decision would later be a comfort and a blessing.

Then, supported by my friends, I was escorted to a room on the trauma side of the emergency room. The lights were low, and it was eerily quiet. Was the room cold, or was it just me in my state of shock? I don't think I will ever know. And there he was, on a cold, sterile-looking gurney with a white sheet draped over him, covering everything but his head and right arm. My friends supported me to the side of the table and held me for several moments. I felt the tears running hot down my face. Then each of my friends, in turn, squeezed my hand or arm and quietly said they would wait outside and give me as long as I needed.

In all my forty-three years, there was nothing I could have done to prepare for the starkness of that moment. There was nothing to do but let the tears fall as I combed my fingers across my husband's balding head and held onto his right hand. The room was so cold; I desperately wanted him to not be cold, but there was nothing except the sheet that lay across his body.

Somehow, I smiled; somehow, I spoke to him softly. "Hi. I'm glad you're not in pain." That might have been the only mercy: that he hadn't survived the accident only to end up permanently injured, irreparably damaged. "I have to tell you," I said, "I'm a little lost right now." *A little.* I couldn't begin to tell him what I felt, but then, no words could ever be enough. "How am I going to move forward?" I tried not to let my words burst out as a sob. "I don't know what to tell the kids. They'll be devasted." Thinking of the grief still to come, I had to brace myself to keep going. "Can you come back to us?" Even as I said it, wishing for it as I had never wished for anything before or since, I knew the answer. "No. I know you would be here if you could; I know you wouldn't want to leave us. "

Then, my words exhausted, I stood there in silence for a long time, tears streaming down my cheeks. "Dave," I finally managed, "when you get to heaven, will you please ask God for a special dose of blessings? I don't know how I'm going to get through whatever comes next. I only know I have to."

I smoothed his hair again and caressed his hand. I had to leave the room, and I didn't want to; I wished I could stay there forever because I was so lost without him. Finally, I leaned over and kissed his forehead. "I don't want to say goodbye," I told him, as bravely as I could, "so I'll just say I love you." I returned his hand beside his still body and willed myself to move toward the door.

My friends met me in the hallway and supported me back to the "crying room." Everything felt like a blur, and yet also so clear; it was almost as though I was watching what was happening to me from a safe distance. I could see that Alicia was taking over in preparation for getting me safely home. My assistant had arrived, and she offered to have her husband help to get my car home. Bill offered to pick up family members from the airport whenever needed. My colleagues assured me that they would handle things at the office. They were all so kind to say whatever I needed, just ask, but I had no idea what I would need in the days, months, and weeks to come.

Alicia walked me to the parking garage where her car was parked.

As I sat down in the passenger seat, an overwhelming fear came over me, and I just kept saying, "How am I going to tell the kids? What am I going to say to them?"

I must have been hysterical because I was not making any sense, so Alicia did the best thing she could at that moment in time. She began to pray. I was so grateful for that single prayer because it gave me the comfort I needed to think a little more clearly.

Alicia had already called her husband Joe, who would meet us at the house so they would both be with me when I told my children. Calls needed to be made to the family; I had already called my mother, who would get in touch with my dad, so that meant I needed to place calls to my husband's parents.

I called his mother first. Nancy and I cried together as I related what had happened. Then I called his father, and as I told him, Harry wailed and said he would have to call me back. I remember thinking that would be fine because I desperately wanted to get off the phone. But I had to make one more call to my brother. It went to voicemail; how do you leave a message about someone dying? Each time I dialed another number, braced myself to speak, I felt my numbness grow. I kept spiraling back to the thought, "How am I going to tell my children?" I cried the entire distance to the house, which was only a few miles, but it felt like forever.

When we pulled into the driveway, I was scared to my core as I'd never been before, almost unable to move. Two hours before, I had told my husband for the last time that I loved him. Now there were three children inside that house who had to be told their father was never coming home again. There were three sets of eyes that would look to me for comfort, strength, and reassurance, none of which I felt or could reach out and touch. How was I going to give them what I did not have myself?

Alicia must have sensed my state because she again prayed for me, and for God's strength and comfort. We walked into the house, and my daughter came to meet us at the door.

Jennifer said, "Mom, what's going on? St. Mary's Hospital called here for you, but they wouldn't tell me anything."

I took her hand and quietly said, "Let's go into the living room with your brothers." The tears had already started as my children looked expectantly at me. "There's been an accident," I said as calmly as I could.

"Where's Daddy?"

"Is Daddy okay?"

"What happened?"

The questions came at me fast from their young voices, and I could hear the fear behind their words, fear that I felt myself but could not let them see. I held them all as I told them what the doctor had told me. How I got through those few moments, I have no idea, other than by the grace of God. The horror in their eyes and voices and their tears broke my heart, and I knew that nothing in our lives would be the same ever again.

We stayed huddled on the living room couch together, just the four of us, for I have no idea how long. Jennifer, the eldest, finally asked if she could go upstairs and call a friend. The boys curled in closer for a few more minutes until Bryan, the middle child, asked if he could go up to his room. The youngest, A.J., crawled up on my lap and just hugged me for a couple of minutes, and then quietly slid down and walked silently to his room. I always loved having the kids curl up in my lap, and at that moment, I wanted nothing but that. A.J.'s heartbeat against my chest meant life, as did the warmth of his little body and tears. Once he left me, I felt utterly alone.

~

In the kitchen, Alicia and Joe had already begun making calls, one of which was to A.J.'s godparents. They were my dear friends, more like my brother and sister. Chris, A.J.'s godmother, showed up shortly after that, as did my husband's cousin, Susan, who lived in nearby Princeton, New Jersey. Between Alicia, Chris, and Susan, whatever needed to be done got done. I can see the activity in my kitchen that day, but it was all directed by others as I sat at the kitchen table, silently crying and trying to do anything but feel the pain of loss. I know that God placed these angels in my presence because that was what I needed at that moment. They also cared for my children, which I was completely unable to do.

I could never have imagined the outpouring of love that came to me over those first days from our church family, friends, neighbors, extended family, family, and colleagues. With the vast majority of my immediate family in Illinois, it was beyond comforting to me to have people nearby who cared. God always provides what we need when we need it. Some people brought food; some people just sat with me and shared fond memories of my husband; some people helped me make phone calls and lists; some people took care of things I could not fathom needed to be done. I have never liked asking for help, but I also know that when help is offered, it is a gift from God; there was nothing I could do but accept it. I still thank God for all those people who cared for us during those early weeks and beyond.

I would like to tell you that it got easier after I told the children, but it did not. Sleep was not my friend that first night, or many after that. Our king size bed seemed much larger than it really was, and it was cold and lonely. I tried to get lost in the bedsheets, but couldn't. Every time I closed my eyes, I saw Dave lying on the gurney in the hospital.

That first night, I took off the crisp professional outfit I'd selected that morning: the sleeveless dress, matching scarf, and navy jacket. They felt like they belonged to someone else, like some other woman had put them on in the morning, so long ago, when her husband was still alive. I held the gold cross Dave had given me and tried to take comfort in its simple shape, and in the memory of his delight on that Christmas twenty-two years before.

Saying Goodbye

I can do all things through him who strengthens me.
Philippians 4:13

The next morning, I woke with numbness throughout my body. My chest felt heavy, and my head ached from lack of sleep, stress, and grief. Even so, it took me a few moments to remember what had happened. Dave got up before me on most mornings, so I was used to waking up by myself, but that morning, I realized how alone I truly was.

I donned my robe and walked to the kitchen. There, I found a friend caring for my kids and talking with my parents, who had arrived as promised. I didn't learn until later that, when I'd called her the day before, my mother had been at a meeting two hours from home. She'd had to drive home and pack before she and my father could get on the road. The fact that they made it to my house in less than eighteen hours from the time I called still amazes me, as it takes at least fourteen hours from their farm to my house. Their generosity was a reminder of the values they had raised me with: that family is the most important thing in life next to God.

As soon as I saw my mother, relief washed over me, though it seemed strange and wrong that I could feel any break from the grief. I knew my mother would take care of the kids and me, so I think I let go of worry the moment I heard her voice and hugged her. As she hugged me back, I cried and cried and cried; she held me tight, as only a loving mother can do. She prayed for me and offered comfort and strength. I couldn't eat anything, though she gently asked. When I refused, she sat with me at the kitchen table and let me talk or stay quiet as I needed to. Years later, I realized how much that morning I wanted my mother to make everything all right again. She couldn't change what had happened, but her presence gave me the help I needed.

~

In many ways, that first day after the accident was harder than the accident itself. More people stopped by the house, I had to have more conversations about what had happened, I had to share more memories of my husband, and so I cried many more tears. I remember feeling numb at all the activity; I needed silence and space, yet at the same time, I felt grateful that I didn't have those things yet.

Someone straightened things up and ran a vacuum; someone made room in the refrigerator for the many dishes that arrived; someone arranged for coolers filled with ice and beverages; someone received flowers and plants, answered the phone, served food to anyone hungry, and cleaned up throughout the day. Someone also took care of my children. Looking back now, I can't even remember what the kids and I said to each other that impossibly long day, or whether we were able to talk at all. All of us, I think, moved blindly along, each carrying our own sadness.

I remember I had to go to the funeral home. The only thing I knew my husband to be adamant about was being cremated rather than buried in a box; I honored those wishes. Dave was a no-frills kind of guy, and in my mind, I heard him say, "just go with the least expensive urn," so that's what I did. The funeral director was very compassionate and worked with me to make all the arrangements.

Thankfully, my mom and Alicia came with me, too, to make some decisions for me that I couldn't handle at that time.

The funeral director suggested we have a family visitation the next day, to say our final goodbyes. I agreed to that blindly, unable to believe it was really going to happen. *Family. Final goodbyes.* The funeral director suggested that my kids and I each write a goodbye to my husband.

"When a loved one is taken suddenly," he explained, "writing a letter can help bring closure, especially with children. If your children want to write letters to their dad and bring them tomorrow, they can leave them with him."

I agreed to suggest that to the kids.

He said, "They can also bring something special between them and their dad that will stay with him for eternity. It can be comforting for young children. It gives them a sense that part of themselves stay with the one who is gone."

I could never have thought of something like that myself. I was grateful for his guidance and insights at a time when I could barely put one foot in front of the other.

When we got back to the house, I just went through the motions. Everything, and I do mean everything, was a blur. Thankfully, my mother, Chris, Susan, and Alicia stepped in an managed all the details. As I look back on that second day, I can honestly say it was the longest day of my life.

Alicia offered to put the memorial service together. I was grateful; I had no idea what to do or what Dave would have wanted. Several family members arrived on Friday and Saturday morning. On Saturday afternoon, those folks, along with extended family, neighbors, and friends, came to the house for a memory session. I don't remember asking people to get together or asking anyone to arrange the session, but it was a blessing.

We talked about our funny memories of Dave, experiences we'd shared with him, and how we would remember him. The kids each shared a favorite memory of their dad. I remember that as each of them talked, they all smiled for the first time in nearly forty-eight hours. All three kids talked about watching the Disneyland sing-a-long video with Dave, and how he'd sung along to *Grim Grinning Ghosts*. Looking back now, I remember exactly how his voice sounded when he sang that song, how he made it deep and gravely so we all would laugh.

I was glad we all had that time together because afterward, we went to the funeral home for the family visitation. Somewhere between twenty and thirty people showed up—family, extended family, and very close friends. I've been asked if I remember people's faces that day, and while it's true that I can picture those faces, what I remember most clearly is the look of shock and sadness we all shared.

We all sat together. One by one, people went up to say goodbye as they were ready. Finally, we had to encourage the kids to go up with the letters they had written for Dave.

Jennifer went on her own, not wanting me to go with her. Bryan tried to go by himself too, but it was too difficult, so he took my hand, and we went together. In his free hand, he held a letter and a base-ball with no covering on which his father had simply written, "Fred." It was a joke they'd shared. Bryan cried as he looked down at his dad's lifeless body. He placed first the letter, then the baseball, on his dad's chest, and said quietly, "You keep it, dad. I love you."

I walked him back to the chair and took A.J. up next. My youngest just cried as he placed his letter and a picture he had drawn on his dad's chest, and then hugged me like he was holding on for dear life. I doubt he remembers it, but I stood there with him on my hip and told my husband that I loved him and already missed him terribly. I asked God to watch over his soul.

We left the funeral home in silence. When we got back to the

THE GIFT OF LOSS

house, we got out all the food and told everyone to help themselves. We were Methodists, and that's what good Methodists do: come together for family and feed everyone. We even managed to joke about it as we set all the food out. So much food: lasagna, roast beef, salads, vegetables, fruit, cakes, loaves of bread. You name it, it was there. Even then, it made me smile to see how we were taking care of each other the way we always did. I remember that spread of food vividly.

～

Over the next two days, people kept coming in and out of the house, and we had more food than you could shake a stick at, but the atmosphere changed a little. We were still very sad, but we were telling stories and finding ourselves able to laugh again. My brother put together a beautiful photo tribute for the memorial service. He set it to "Wish You Were Here" by Pink Floyd, one of my husband's all-time favorite bands. It made me smile to think that it was probably the first and last time Pink Floyd would be played inside a church.

I still don't remember how I got through the day of the memorial service. Family, extended family, and friends helped me: God truly sent his angels that day. I learned later that nearly 400 people attended the service. Dave was a very outgoing person, but that turnout still amazed me: my co-workers, members of the bank's board of directors, fellow chamber members, former co-workers, clients, neighbors, fellow church members, friends, and family. I stood at the front of the church and greeted each one of them. I cried and laughed, shook hands, and hugged.

After the luncheon the church put on, for which I'm still thankful from the bottom of my heart, I remember thinking, "Now what, God?" I had absolutely no idea what I should do next, what plans I needed to make, what details I had to attend to. Nothing.

My powerlessness panicked me. I think most people thought I was just sad, but I was paralyzed. I was a parent, a business leader;

I was used to making decisions. Suddenly, I felt as if I didn't know anything at all.

Are contractors coming to work on the house? How do I clean the pool filter? Do I need to order heating oil? What's up in the attic, and what do I do with it? Do I know how to start the lawnmower? The simplest questions threw me. Fortunately, my parents kept their heads and began to guide me to think about certain things. I needed to attend to the estate, which meant I needed to file certain papers, make changes with the bank, cancel credit cards, and get my will in order. Concrete details of how to go on living after loss.

The list went on from there. We had to contact the kids' schools and let them know what had happened, as the school year would begin in only two and a half weeks. It felt surreal to think about things like, *Whose name do I put down as an emergency contact for the kids? Who will take care of them after school while I'm at work?* Dave had always been the contact; Dave had always been the caregiver as he worked from home. I tried to think about how I would get the kids to school in the mornings without help. I still couldn't believe I would be doing that alone.

Then there were the home improvement projects that my husband had been working on. I needed to contact the contractors and figure out where each project stood. *Is someone coming to work on something at the end of this week?* I had no idea. They had all been Dave's projects; he had devoted his attention to them and developed strong relationships with the contractors he'd chosen. I knew I could trust those people, but I didn't know who they were or any of the information about what they were doing. I managed to find a few notes Dave had written down about each project, but I couldn't find everything.

In the end, I had to realize I could only handle one thing at a time, take care of each question as it came up. I could only do the best I could. I knew, even then, that maybe I should have paid more attention to our home life; maybe I should have stayed more tapped into what Dave was working on, and shouldn't have taken so many things for granted. You might think I felt angry at Dave for leaving me to handle it all by myself, but I didn't. I just felt baffled that I hadn't realized how many important details made up our life together.

Going Home

Do not let your hearts be troubled.
You believe in God; believe also in me.
My Father's house has many rooms; if that were not so,
would I have told you that I am going there
to prepare a place for you?
John 14:1-2

Eleven days after our tragedy, my parents packed the children and me into their van. We drove fourteen hours to the family farm in Illinois, where my children could bask in more family love, and I could simply rest.

The farm was familiar; it was home. As we drove into the driveway, I breathed a sigh of relief for the first time in two weeks. In the corner of my mind, I knew I still had grown-up responsibilities, but just for a few days, someone else would take care of things.

The farmhouse, a beige and brown ranch-style with three bedrooms, full basement, and a one-car garage, sat on five acres with the front-facing north. Flowers, bushes, and trees grew in the front yard, and my mother had planted flowers along the side of the garage, which was on the west end of the house. More flowers adorned the deck at the back of the house, just off the kitchen. The kids had made stepping-stones back there too, and Mom had built up a collection of raccoon statues in honor of the family name,

Coons. Dave always loved looking for statues to give my mom.

The house felt like *home* to me, comfortable and safe. Settling in there, I began to deal with some of the questions swirling in my head. I'd heard kids are resilient and bounce back, but could my children do that, after the loss they had just sustained? Would this trip to the farm help them? Would it help them to move forward? What could I do to help them be resilient? How could I make things right for them? So many questions that I couldn't answer, that I didn't know how to express to anyone.

My mom always made sure her home was warm and inviting. As I tried to recover myself and put the pieces of my life back together, I let myself sink into the memories of the old house.

The dining and living rooms were both large and open, with cathedral ceilings. There was a sofa that divided the two spaces, and in front of the sofa, there was a neat oak coffee table with two layers. One layer swiveled to expand the surface area. There was something calming in shaping the table into different positions. Family photos hung over the piano on the west wall; my mom always called that collection our "rogues' gallery." The living room also held a large entertainment center and three wall units full of books, collectibles, and sheet music. I had many memories of playing the piano and sitting down to games with my brother in that room.

The master bedroom and my room were on the east side of the house, farthest away from the garage. My brother's room was just off the kitchen. When my parents built the house, they let my brother and me pick out the carpeting and colors for our rooms, so I went with brightly-colored, sculptured shag carpet; my eleven-year-old self thought that was the coolest. My white desk and dresser were still as they had been when I was a kid. My father had made the bulletin board that hung on the wall, which I'd filled with some photos, buttons, and ribbons. My sons slept in my bedroom now, in the two twin beds my parents had put in.

I slept in one of the two bedrooms my parents had added to the house when they'd finished the basement a few years before. The new bedrooms were nothing fancy, good beds, and simple amenities. The concrete walls were still visible, but they were homey for sure. The other new bedroom was Jennifer's home base while we visited. I liked the new space, but I also remembered the unfinished basement of my childhood, with a pool table and so much space I could have gone roller-skating in it.

The kitchen was definitely the hub of the house, right in the middle of the floor plan. It was large, open, and bright, filled with smells of whatever foods were being prepared; sweet, savory, and always delicious. Every family event we'd ever had, from my earliest memories through my adulthood, had involved that kitchen. The expandable oak table near the window had belonged to my grandmother. It had seen many family meals over the years. I'd learned to cook in my mom's kitchen. It had changed very little over the years; all my memories were there to welcome me back.

~

During that stay in my parents' house, no one pushed me to do anything I wasn't ready to do. I was grateful to be left alone, but at the same time, I remember how surreal and numb everything felt. I was part of what was going on around me, but on some level, I also wasn't. I remember crying when the kids were not around. I didn't want them to see me less than what they needed from me, but thinking back, I'm sure they knew I was hurting as much as they were.

The farm offered them some distractions. Grandpa had things that the boys could do to keep them busy: feed the kitties in the barn, crush cans for recycling, take care of the garden, play outside. They were small day-to-day activities, but they brought some normalcy back into Bryan's and A.J.'s lives. Jennifer helped with household chores and spent time reading. The kids smiled once in a while and laughed a little; it was good to hear their laughter when they let it come through.

Each of the kids needed me as much as the next, yet each one needed something a little different. Sometimes it was just a hug or watching a movie or going into town for a coke. Other times they needed to talk about things. They needed to go over, again, what had happened to their dad, and they needed my reassurances that we were going to be okay. None of them had been what I'd call clingy, but I think we hugged more those first few weeks than we otherwise might have. I know I told them I loved them more often. I desperately wanted to make things okay for them.

One day during our visit, I went to Hobby Lobby with my mother to buy yarn so I could crochet an afghan. I needed something to keep me busy, so I did not go mad from the numbness. Years before, my grandmothers had taught me how to crochet, and by the time I was 16, I was pretty good.

Over the years, I had made many blankets and other items, always with a person or purpose in mind. I'd been making prayer shawls most recently, so I decided this would be a good time to make a prayer afghan. It would take a lot longer to complete, which meant it would keep my mind occupied, so I didn't have to think about the pain and loneliness I was experiencing.

On that trip to Hobby Lobby, I chose colors of yarn that made me smile: muted, soft hues of blue, mauve, green, and ivory. I found a pattern I liked, one that had a lot of repetition so I didn't have to think too hard as I crocheted. If you crochet or knit, you know that before you begin, you prepare by setting the scene. I chained the foundation and got into a rhythm, and as I counted stitches, I prayed. The repetition and the melodic tone in my mind were comforting, almost relaxing. I had never thought about crocheting being a meditative process, but at that point in my life, that's exactly what it was. I prayed for comfort and strength for my children to be okay, for our lives to be right again. As I kept my hands busy, I cried, but only if I was alone. Sometimes I was lucid and conscious of what I was creating, but other times, my fingers moved on their own as my mind concentrated on the prayer. I'm amazed that the stitches were consistent and even when it was finally finished.

~

All through that stay in Illinois, I thought about Dave. Memories filled my mind of times when we had all been to the farm together, the last time having been the previous Christmas. I thought about all the things we'd planned to do in the years to come. I cried for the fact that we would never travel to Hawaii for our twentieth anniversary, as we'd expected to do, and that we would never celebrate fifty years of marriage, as my grandparents and great aunt and uncle had done, and as my parents soon would. Often, I felt as though I was watching the scenes of my life from a cloud.

I remember family visiting, offering support and love but not really knowing what to say. I think I may have laughed a bit that week, but I'm really not sure. I do remember seeing people who had known me since I was a child in the small town where I had grown up, and I remember accepting their kind words regarding our loss.

One night, my parents wanted to attend the high school football game as my cousin's son was playing, so we all went to the game. The kids sat with their cousins and grandpa while my mom and I sat in the car on the sidelines. I crocheted because I really wasn't interested in the game. Classmates I hadn't seen in years, and family friends stopped by the car to say hello and see how I was holding up.

"Hi, Cathy. I'm really sorry for your loss. How are you doing?"

"Thank you. I'm about as well as I can be," I'd reply.

"How are the kids doing?"

"They're struggling," I'd say, "but they'll find their way. We all will."

On the outside, I tried to look like I had it together. On the inside, I wanted to scream at them. *Don't you understand I just lost my husband, and I have no idea what to do now?*

I was scared! I had been scared before, true, but never like this. This was very different from being afraid I wouldn't pass a test or be able to withstand childbirth or find a job. Now I was scared to my core because I had no previous experience to draw from that told me everything would eventually be okay. I withdrew into myself. I didn't sleep much. I would put my head on the pillow and close my eyes, but memories and visions took over and sucked all the hope from my heart. I never felt rested, and blackness surrounded me. Soon, I knew, I was going to get on a plane to fly back to Pennsylvania with three fatherless children and without my parents to help me, and I had absolutely no idea how I was going to do it.

I would have to pay the bills: the mortgage, utilities, the scheduled home improvement projects. I remember thanking God that the car was paid off. One less thing to worry about. How was I going to work full-time and care for the children's needs? My job demanded that I put in long hours, and the kids were in three different schools. How was I going to manage the different schedules and activities? Dave and I used to barely do it with two of us, but now it was just me. I was afraid of everything, sometimes even my own shadow.

I didn't think I could let anyone see how scared I was. I tried to remember all the organization and time management skills I had learned, so I'd be able to put systems in place to keep tabs on the kids when I was not with them, even if I knew who was caring for them. I tried to promise myself I could control how everything would pan out. If I couldn't, I thought, the fear would paralyze me.

God sends angels exactly when we need them. "Touch me, O Lord, and fill me with your light and hope. Give me strength when I am weak, courage when I am afraid, comfort when I am alone, hope when I feel rejected, and peace when I am in turmoil. Amen."

I had many conversations with God during those first days, not one of which I remember with any clarity. But with each conversation came mercy and exactly what and who I needed for whatever was happening. I had no idea what I needed, but God did, and he provided in so many ways.

I have to acknowledge all those people who prayed for us. I can honestly say that I have no idea how I got through it all, except that my faith helped me, and the prayers that were lifted on our behalf by scores of people I don't even know. Every time I thought I could not go on, I felt those prayers lifting me, comforting and strengthening me so I could continue to put one foot in front of the other. For every single person who ever prayed for my children and me, whether it was in the first few days or in the subsequent weeks and months that followed, I thank you from the bottom of my heart. You were one of the angels sent when I needed you most.

A New Normal

Do not be anxious about anything, but in everything by prayer and supplication with thanksgiving, let your requests be made known to God. And the peace of God, which surpasses all understanding will guard your hearts and your minds in Christ Jesus.
Philippians 4:6

That Labor Day weekend, the kids and I returned to Pennsylvania, and we began to find a "new normal." It was very surreal being in the house without my husband those first few weeks. I can't tell you how many times I would enter a room and expect to see him there. I would answer the phone and hear his voice even though it was someone else speaking. I would walk into the garage and hear his laugh. I would sit at the kitchen table and say something, waiting for him to answer. I would come home at the end of a long day, expecting to meet him in the kitchen and tell him about my day, only to be disappointed he wasn't there. The air itself felt thick, like fog, when I would forget and then remember that he wasn't there to do or say something.

Nights were the worst because once the kids were in bed, the house was quiet. Some nights I would watch television alone for hours, just to keep from going to bed and seeing Dave in the hospital or the funeral home, or imagining the scene of the accident. Some nights I cried myself to sleep, if I slept at all. And then I would have to get up the next morning and do it all over again. Those first weeks, I found myself thinking often, *it's not fair.* And then I would hear myself saying, "Sometimes, life just isn't fair."

When school started, friends and family came together to help where my kids and I needed it. Mornings in our house were chaotic at first, mostly because I didn't want to get out of bed and be an adult. When I finally would, I had to rush to get out the door on time for work, which meant I would hustle the boys out of bed, a difficult feat most mornings because they only wanted to go back to sleep. Dave used to use an acronym to get the boys up; he would tell them to "FOF and BOB," which meant "feet on the floor and butt out of bed." I used to think it was silly, but after about a month of saying it myself and having it work, I thought it was a nice tool to help mornings go a little smoother.

Our friends Tim and Kathy stepped in to help with our daily routine; a blessing for sure. Tim would get to the house around seven in the morning to help get the boys ready for school. Breakfast was usually cereal or "regular" pop tarts as the kids called them. They were brown sugar cinnamon, bought by the case at Sam's Club. (I'm so sorry, kids; I didn't know any better back then!)

After school, Tim would be there to make sure all three kids got home and got homework started. Some days he would play games with them or run errands; some days, they watched movies. Most days, I didn't get home until 6 pm or later, so sometimes Tim would help the kids start dinner or even have dinner ready when I came home. What a blessing that was! We would usually sit down to dinner together; I insisted that my kids and I have at least dinner time to connect and talk. Once or twice a week, Joe and Alicia and their kids, or Chris and Rich, or all of them, would join us. Having people join us for dinner somehow made it seem easier to handle the fact that our family was fractured.

Joe and Rich came to my rescue with the various contractor projects, and then helped make sure all the work got done the way

Dave had intended. Another Godsend! During all of this, sometimes I wondered why I wasn't angry at Dave, why I didn't scream. *Why did you leave me alone?* But I didn't; I was more sad than anything. He wouldn't see it all come to fruition the way he had planned. He had planned everything so carefully that I remember wondering one time if he had organized things that way just in case. I found myself smiling at that thought. Dave was an Eagle Scout through and through: "be prepared."

Joe and Alicia and Chris and Rich always seemed to know just what to say and do to make me feel as though everything was going to be all right. Meals were prepared and dropped off at the house from time to time, and the kids had car rides to activities and appointments after school, so I didn't have to always take off work. We received help in so many ways. I was grateful because it gave me space to figure out my next move, or at least, that's what I thought I was doing.

~

About three months after the tragic events that set my life on a new trajectory, I was at work and realized everything—and I do mean everything!—had become too overwhelming. Working my own job, making sure the kids got their homework done, keeping normalcy in the house, paying bills, cooking, cleaning, laundry, getting out of bed in the morning, putting on a brave face, keeping up with things at work and church. You name it, everything had become too much.

I had thought that keeping myself as busy as I could possibly be would make me feel alive, living. I'd thought all of that activity would push the emptiness out of me. But, three months after Dave's death, I found myself walking into a colleague's office and collapsing. I babbled about being in over my head, how I couldn't take the pressure of raising kids and working, and trying to meet everyone else's expectations. I must have been more hysterical than I realized because shortly after that, the vice president of human resources came to my office, closed the door, and asked me to come to sit at the table with her. We chatted, and she shared her story of loss with me and how counseling helped her get through it. I was not sure counseling was right for me, but she suggested I give it a try. The bank's employee benefits included therapy. I finally agreed to make an appointment. It was helpful to talk with someone who was not biased, someone who simply listened and asked questions. After six weeks, I thought I felt better and discontinued therapy.

~

During this time, Jennifer grew up faster than she should have had to. She had a strong core group of friends to support her every step of the way, but she felt the need to stay closer to home to help with her brothers. Most mornings, she woke to her alarm and was out the door before 6:30 am to catch the bus to school.

That first year was her freshman year of high school. She had always been an excellent student, and her dad insisted she have a good education, so in the spring before he died, they had planned her freshman course schedule together. One day, she came home from school and said that nothing felt right about her schedule because dad wasn't there to go through it with her.

"We planned my classes together so he could be part of what I was learning," she said. "Now, it just seems stupid and hard."

Wow! What do you say to your fourteen-year-old daughter when she's right? Life had thrown us all a big curveball. Her world had collapsed, and school didn't really mean anything at that point. "Well," I said. "Did Daddy help you pick classes where you already knew everything or ones where you could learn and would have to put some effort into?"

She looked at me and thought about this. "Ones where I would have to put in some effort."

"And was he going to do the work for you, or just be your cheerleader to do your best?"

She thought about this too. "Be my cheerleader."

I asked her, "Don't you think, then, that you owe it to yourself and Daddy's memory to do your best? He wouldn't want you to stop learning just because he isn't here to help you, right?"

"I guess not," she said.

I held her hand and smiled. "That's right," I said. "He would want you to keep learning and growing, no matter how hard it was. He always thought you should learn something new every day, so how about you keep doing that? I know he's looking down on you now and cheering you on."

Yes, Jennifer grew up quickly that year. She wasn't responsible for her brothers, but she did a lot to help me care for them and the house. I couldn't do it all alone, so I relied on her more than I probably should have. Sometimes, I had to remind myself that she was still a teenager and needed to do her own thing.

I believe in the power of positivity, always have. Even at the lowest times in my life, I have tried to find the positive in every situation. I will admit that sometimes this isn't an easy task, and sometimes I've succumbed and let negativity creep in, probably more than I even know. Thankfully, I have always been surrounded by people who love me: my parents, my family, my friends. They have surrounded me with their actions, kind words, and guidance, reinforcing the Golden Rule about striving to love others as I love myself.

Although I didn't always know it as I was going through it, that's exactly what was taking place in me during those first months after Dave's death. At first, I constantly struggled with disbelief: how had my life changed so fast? One minute I was happy, the next I was devastatingly sad. How do you find positivity in that? I never questioned God or asked, *Why me?* because I somehow knew I was being cared for. I have to admit I also didn't want to hear, "Why not you?" Some days, I thought things were better: I even smiled and laughed a little.

Then, other days, the feeling of being overwhelmed was so great I would cry. Not very positive.

Some people thought they were helping when they made comments like, "Only the good die young, and "Just give it time, "or Time heals all wounds," and "Everything happens for a reason." And my favorite comment: "God must have needed him in heaven." Let me give you a little insight here. If you are ever talking with someone who is grieving, don't offer any of these platitudes. Instead, do what my family and dear friends did for me: offer love. Pure, simple, heartfelt love. It's a much more positive and supportive approach.

Right before our first Thanksgiving without Dave, I got a strong reminder of the power of positivity and the impact it could have. Many people sent me cards and notes during the first couple of months, but slowly, they tapered off. Except for one couple from my church, who seemed to send me at least one card a week.

The Sunday before Thanksgiving, our church service focused on gratitude and telling people what you were grateful for. We talked about sharing and caring and thanking those people who had an impact on you in the past year. I was truly grateful for all the love and support my kids and I had received, but at the same time, I was feeling pretty low because I didn't know how to be grateful when I was so sad. Then I saw Hap and Jean after the service. They were the couple who had been sending me cards for months, cards that always touched my heart. Something inside nudged me to visit with Jean a little bit, so I did.

She hugged me. When I asked her how she was doing, she smiled her wonderfully warm smile and said, "I'm just fine. The day is sunny, and it's a gift. How are you, my dear?"

"I'm hanging in there, I guess," I said. Jean was always so kind, asked how we all were, and truly cared about the answer.

"Each day is a gift. Give yourself time and take each day as it comes. You're a strong woman and a good mother, and God is on your side," Jean said.

"Thank you, I'll try to remember that. May I ask you a question?"

"Of course."

"Please know that I'm very grateful for each of the cards you send me, but I'm wondering why you keep sending them."

Jean smiled and put her hand on my arm as she said, "We send each of those cards because it's the best we can do to let you know we support, pray and care for you and the children. This is our ministry. We want you to know that you're in our prayers and thoughts. It's just our way of letting you know that you are cared for."

I had tears at the corners of my eyes as I listened. I thanked her for sharing their ministry with me, both in the receiving and the explaining. It was a beautiful expression of love and care, one that I will always cherish.

~

When I was in high school, I was introduced to a book about positive mental attitude that has always stuck with me. It told me that when we find the positive in each situation rather than the negative, we can see possibilities.

Encouragement and positivity go hand in hand. Two of my strong supports were my Sunday School class and small group Bible study at church as I felt safe and encouraged to see the positive in every situation. So many people walked with me through the worst times. Eileen and Jan always had a kind word and always had an encouraging scripture to share with me.

The love and support of my friends and family always pulled me back to the edge of positivity. I didn't always understand it, but each time I came back from the negative side of life, I found a new opportunity to be grateful.

Thanksgiving has always been one of my favorite times of the year. I was so glad to have my parents with us for that first Thanksgiving, but it was very hard for me to be truly thankful. We gathered with friends. Once again, I put on a brave face, even though

I was in pain on the inside. I thanked God for all that we had and for all the love we had received, but I knew something was missing.

It had always been our tradition to take the kids out and get a Christmas tree shortly after Thanksgiving. That year, I couldn't do it. I couldn't lift the tree on my own. I couldn't put it in the stand. Even if I could have gotten the tree into the house, I didn't know how I would get it out after the holidays. I needed to make changes that would work for me, so I wouldn't have to depend on anyone but the kids and me to get decorations up and down. An artificial tree was in order.

Once I made that decision, I began to think about the decorations. Dave had always liked decorating the tree, and we had amassed quite a collection of ornaments over the years. As the kids and I pulled the boxes out of the attic, I began to cry. I couldn't put up all the tree ornaments that he had loved so much. I didn't want to make the kids sad, but I needed to make new traditions that fit our new normal. I had always wanted a Precious Moments tree, so I got a few new ornaments to go with all Precious Moments ornaments I had collected over the years and prayed that would make Christmas okay.

As I shopped for presents that year, I was meticulous about picking things out and making sure that each child had the same number of gifts to open on Christmas morning. I did everything in my power to make the holiday full and wonderful to keep the kids from feeling sad that their dad wasn't there. I even planned a trip with my parents to Hershey Park so the kids would have fun memories that year. Even though I said it was all for the kids, I, too, needed new memories, new traditions, new directions to keep me from hurting. It was only a Band-Aid, a temporary cure. Strengthening myself in positivity was the real cure.

When we live in negativity, fear is the driving force behind each decision we make. We tend to be pessimistic and walk around with a cloud over our heads. Negativity finds all the reasons something will not work and is fearful of every encounter, big or small.

When we live in positivity, possibilities abound. Gratitude is the driving force for living and decision making. We live our lives looking for the good and embracing the opportunities because we understand that opportunity does not knock twice. Positivity finds reasons to be grateful, big or small.

There is a saying that I recently saw again after several years that I think is wonderful. "Don't let negative people hang out in your mind. They don't pay rent and they drain your energy because they always want something from you. Increase the rent and they'll go away."

Wow! If I don't want to be surrounded by negative people, I just have to "raise my rent": raise my game and standards. Makes perfect sense, but how does one actually make that happen?

First, you have to embrace positivity. Make a choice to be happy, be positive. Try it in small steps, maybe an hour or two a day, where you are nothing but positive. Write down what you do, how you feel about what you have done, and how others respond to you. After a few days, increase your positive time to half a day, and then after a few days, increase it to a whole day. Pretty soon, you will be living a more positive life, and my guess is you'll be loving it.

One of the things I did to raise my positivity quotient is gratitude. Each day, I find at least three things for which to be grateful. I try really hard to not repeat things for at least a month so that by the end of thirty days, I find I have been grateful for at least ninety blessings in my life. I also write them down so I can review them periodically and always continue to be grateful for what I have and who I am. It is much easier to love yourself – and others – when you are continually thankful, but it is also much easier to stay focused on self-care because you are reinforcing your self-worth through your gratitude.

ARKs

Share with the Lord's people who are in need.
Practice hospitality. Bless those who persecute you;
bless and do not curse. Rejoice with those who rejoice;
mourn with those who mourn. Live in harmony with one another.
Romans 12:13-16

Another way to increase my positivity quotient has been through kindness. It takes less effort to be kind than to be unkind, so why would you want to expend more negative energy? Kindness is a simple way to raise your positivity. Saying "please" and "thank you" (the magic words, don't you know), acknowledging someone for a good job, letting someone in front of you in line at the grocery store, or allowing a car to merge in front of you in traffic are all acts of kindness. Kindness is always in style, and it is so easy to offer. You never know what another person is going through, and your act of kindness might be the one positive that turns their day from bad to good.

ARKs (acts of random kindness) are also a great way to increase positivity. ARKs are wonderful because they can be spontaneous and are unexpected by the recipient. They can be big and small. They can involve money or not. They can be seen or unseen. The most important thing about ARKs is that they are done with no expectation of repayment or acknowledgment.

I cannot begin to tell you the number of ARKs I received that first year. I had to learn to receive, rather than provide. I never thought of myself as needing help, but that first Christmas, I was overwhelmed by the kindness of strangers and people who wished to remain anonymous. I remember that Christmas Eve, after the kids had gone to bed, a bag was delivered to my front door. My parents and I were sitting in the living room, and by the time I got up to answer the door (which was only a few seconds), there was no one in sight, just a large bag filled with gifts for the children.

I quickly went to the street to see who was driving away, but there weren't any cars out there. I looked around the corner of the house to see who might be hiding in the shadows but still saw no one. I listened to hear a door shut or a car drive off in the distance, but the cold night air held nothing but silence. I even looked into the sky to see what might be up there, because we have a saying in our house—"if you don't believe, you don't receive." No, I didn't see anything flying in the sky, but at that moment, the offered kindness comforted me.

As I continued to heal, I began to focus on how I might perform acts of kindness for others. At the time of Dave's death, our whole family was involved in a ministry at our church called Angel Food Ministries. It was a food program through which people could purchase a box of food full of fresh, frozen, and staple foods to feed a family of four for two weeks. The paperwork Dave brought me on the day of the accident was for this ministry. The kids and I continued to participate in the ministry team for the five years it was at our church.

Sometimes my ARKs were smaller and more personal. I paid for coffee for someone in line behind me. I left gift cards at the grocery store to pay for someone in need. I let people merge in line before me, even when I had been sitting in traffic for longer than I wanted to. I wanted ARKs always to be part of my life in both directions.

I've found other ways to increase my positivity too. Music is one. I have an eclectic musical taste: everything from musicals to jazz, easy listening to pop, rock 'n roll to top 40, and even a little country (with emphasis on little). I like a wide range of artists. Sometimes I like to just listen, sometimes I dance to the music, and sometimes I sing along, but I always let the music touch my soul and inspire. When the music touches my soul, I can't help but smile: and that makes me happy.

Smiling is another way to increase my positivity quotient. Can you believe it? Something so simple as smiling can help you live a more positive life. Smiling can also increase your ability to laugh, which in turn improves your immune function, so the question becomes, why would you not smile...and smile often?

Sometimes, life balance can be extremely simple. Simply making a choice to live in positivity rather than negativity can bring peace and contentment to your life.

Learning to live in self-care is not as easy as it seems. In fact, it takes hard work and time to make self-care your lifestyle. I know because I have lived it, fought it, and finally embraced it, so I can speak from experience and the heart.

It took me several years, after the loss of my husband, to realize how much more I could do and even needed to do for myself. After Jennifer went to college, and Bryan and Andrew became more independent, I began to realize I needed to exercise my brain more for me, instead of always focusing just on the kids. I had always been active in my career, very creative, organized, and results-oriented, yet as I considered what I might do going forward, I quickly realized I didn't want to go back to corporate America or do marketing consulting again.

I realized I needed to find a way and make a new beginning for myself. First, though, my children and I had more challenges to face.

Cracked Open

And call on me in the day of trouble;
And I will deliver you, and you will honor me.
Psalm 50:15

That first year without Dave was difficult. I felt as though I should be feeling "better" with every milestone that passed, but I didn't. By the time we came to the first anniversary of Dave's death, I was wound pretty tight. The kids and I bought a tree to plant at the church in Dave's memory, but the day I went to pick out a tree was another ARK for sure. I ran into the contractor who had just completed the front landscaping (Dave had selected him, of course).

"How are you doing, Cathy?" he said. "How's the yard?"

"Okay," I replied. "The front yard looks great. The kids still tease me because I water my rocks." We both laughed because when he'd put in the large, decorative rocks, he had told the kids they were just like the plants to add life to the look.

"What are you looking for today?" he asked. "Do you need more flowers planted?"

"No, nothing like that," I said. I explained I was on my lunch hour and wanted to pick out a tree to plant at the church for Dave. "The one-year anniversary is in two weeks, and we want to get the tree planted before that. We're having a small memorial service on the tenth."

"What kind of tree are you looking for?" he asked.

I had to admit I didn't know. How do you decide what kind of tree is just right in this situation? "I want something that'll have some character and color in the different seasons, and I want something that will grow strong, but not super big."

He asked where the tree was going to be planted and then directed me to some maple trees. He suggested two different ones and explained why and which one he would select if it was his decision. I finally decided on a red maple.

"How are you going to get this to the church?" he asked.

"I was going to have them deliver it for me, I guess."

"Why don't you let me take care of that for you?" he said. "I'd be honored to do that." And he did just that.

I called Joe and Alicia to let them know the plan and arranged to meet them at the church in a couple of hours to plant the tree.

At this same time, I'd been working on a big community day event for church. We were trying to figure out how to make smoothies for the event and actually turn a profit on them. I rushed home from work that afternoon, so I could put a smoothie recipe together for everyone to taste-test while we planted the tree. I was rushed to get ready, the boys were rambunctious, and Jennifer, who'd been baby-sitting them all day, was on edge. None of us was looking forward to going to the church to plant the tree, but we knew we needed to do it.

Picture the chaotic scene in my kitchen. I had all the smoothie ingredients out, and as I put them in the blender, I'm pleading with the kids to get ready to go, so we're not late to meet Joe and Alicia. I turned around to say something to Jennifer and then turned back to turn on the blender. You guessed it: I forgot to put the lid on before hitting blend. Everything in the blender splattered all over the kitchen: floor, walls, ceiling, appliances, everywhere. I'm not sure if there was more on the kids and me or on the paint and furniture. I stood there for a moment, trying to decide if I should scream, cry, or laugh.

Before I could make up my mind, Jennifer laughed. "Oh no!" she said through giggles. "Just laugh, Mom." She smiled at me. "Just laugh and let it go."

I looked at her in disbelief. Now I had to clean the kitchen before we could leave, and we were already running behind.

And just as quickly as I had that thought, I began to laugh. I laughed so hard I cried. The kids laughed too and started poking fun at me.

Then, with tears in her eyes, Jennifer said, "You know, Dad did that same thing one time. He would have laughed and laughed if he were here. Don't you think it's good for us to laugh too?"

Out of the mouths of babes. She was right! Dave would have laughed hysterically over that scene. It did lighten the mood for what we all knew was to come, and that somehow made the rest of that day a little more bearable.

We made it through the first-anniversary memorial service with the help of family and friends. I thought I had weathered the storm. Little did I know what was just around the corner.

~

A couple of months later, I was confronted with another curveball, one that involved my daughter and one of her friends.

We were attending a Boy Scout Court of Honor at the church on a beautiful fall Sunday afternoon. One of my girl scouts (I had been the leader for the troop at the church for a few years) and a friend of my daughter's asked to talk with me. She prefaced our conversation by saying, "Promise me you won't tell my parents about what we discuss."

"I can't promise that, Lauren. What I can promise you is I will listen without judgment, and if it's something your parents need to know, I'll go with you to tell them."

She thought about that for a minute and then agreed. "What constitutes sexual assult?" she asked.

"Has someone hurt you or touched you inappropriately?" I asked.

"If you mean touching my breasts, then yes," she replied.

"First of all, it is never acceptable for someone to touch you without your permission. Period. Now, tell me exactly what happened and when."

Lauren told that a member of the church, the father of one of their friends, would touch and fondle her during the worship service as well as church and youth events. As I listened, my anger grew as my heart constricted. Our church had always been a safe haven, no matter what. I was as dumbfounded as I was disgusted.

I asked a few more questions as my mind raced with what the next steps would be. I then asked, "Is there anyone else who knows about this?"

"Yes, Jennifer. She didn't want you to know, but I want to know how to stop it because it doesn't make me feel good," Lauren said.

I couldn't believe it! What? Had I just hear her correctly? Now I had to deal with this on two levels: one as a leader in the church and one as a mother of a victim. "You did the right thing talking with me. Thank you for trusting me. Now I think you need to tell your mom. She will understand just as I did, and she won't be angry with you. I'll go with you if you want, but you need to tell her because I have to take this to the pastor."

How's that for a light Sunday afternoon conversation? I couldn't believe what I heard, especially when I learned that in my daughter's case, the sexual assault had been going on for four years. How could this have happened when Dave and I were both right there to look after Jennifer? How could it have happened when our whole family had felt safe at church, so beloved and at home?

When I composed myself enough to talk with Jennifer calmly, I asked her why she never told us.

"Mom," she said simply, "if I had ever told Daddy, I know he would have killed the guy. I didn't want my dad to go to jail."

That made sense coming from a young girl, but I asked, "So why didn't you tell me, especially when it kept happening after Daddy was gone?"

She looked at me with tears in her eyes. "Because I'd just lost one parent. I didn't want to lose the only parent I had left."

Talk about a punch in the gut. I wanted to be the momma bear who could protect her cub at all costs, and yet, right then, I knew my girl was right. There's no telling what I'd have done or tried to do if she had brought this awful news to me when we were all reeling from Dave's death. Right then, as I tried to make sense of what we had to do next, all I could offer her was a hug.

I can't begin to tell you how angry I was. How could this happen to my baby girl? How could someone we knew do this? As we began the process to deal with what had happened, we found that Jennifer and Lauren hadn't been the man's only victims. Once the pastor got involved, the police and victim's assistance came in, and we found that 33 women and girls were affected by this man's behavior.

After nearly seven months of interviews by the police and prosecutors, it came time for the preliminary hearing. Jennifer and Lauren, surrounded by family and several members of our church family, went to court to testify. We waited in the conference room. We prayed and talked and laughed until the prosecutor came in.

"Ladies, thank you for hanging in there while we went through some formalities with the judge," the prosecutor said. He explained that they could move forward with three felony counts of sexual assault and several misdemeanors, or they could drop the felony charges to misdemeanors, and the accused would plead guilty and be sentenced to county jail; no testifying for the latter. "It's up to you how we proceed, but I will tell you if we go for the felony charges, we can only use Jennifer's testimony at this point." He left the room so we could discuss what the girls wanted to do.

After discussion and tears, the girls decided to allow the prosecutor to lessen the charges and be done. The thought of being the only one to testify was frightening, and I was proud of my daughter for making a very grown-up decision. Somehow, it was enough to know that this predator would be behind bars.

Once again, I came through that time by the grace of God.

Several weeks later, we went to the county courthouse for the sentencing hearing. I cried when I stood before the judge to give my own testimony. I had friends around me, but the grief and anger were too much.

"You were welcomed into our home when my husband was killed," I said, speaking straight to the accused.

He stood behind the defense table dressed in an orange jump-suit and in shackles looking like he'd lost his best friend; his court-appointed attorney stood next to him.

He looked at me as I said, "We greeted you with love and kindness every time we attended a church event together. We stood by and helped you and your family during difficult times. Our daughters are friends. How you could take advantage of my daughter is something I will never understand."

As I went on, he dropped his head and avoided making eye contact with me. "As God is my witness," I said, "I will never forget what you have done and how you have taken away part of my daughter's innocence. I will forgive you because that's what Christ tells me I need to do. Your judgment will be from Him, not me. As it says in Romans 12:19, '...never take revenge. Leave that to the righteous anger of God. For the scriptures say, "I will take revenge; I will pay them back," says the Lord.'

"You have sinned against my daughter, my family, and my husband's memory, but more importantly, you have sinned against God. You will have to live with your demons. Know that I trust in God and this judge to punish you accordingly, and be thankful that I am not in their shoes."

As I took my seat, the judge shook his head in empathy. He told the accused he should listen to the gracious words just spoken and take them to heart. He then asked if the accused had anything to say before his sentence was announced.

"Your Honor," he said, "I'm sorry."

The judge interrupted him, saying, "Stop right there. Don't apologize to me. You need to apologize to the people you hurt, the woman who gave you such grace just now."

Crying, the accused turned toward us and said, "I'm sorry."

The judge agreed that the accused's actions were despicable, and said he wished the law allowed for a more severe sentence, but he could only impose the maximum allowed by law: three years followed by five years probation, be registered as a sex offender, required to take a sex offenders course, never have contact with any of his victims, and no trespassing on church property.

As I listened to the judge, I felt both appalled and relieved; Jennifer was simply relieved it was over. Did I feel sorry for the man? Maybe a tiny, tiny bit. Mostly, I felt sorry for his family—a wife and five children—who were just as affected as our family was. Although the man was physically alive, I knew the pain of loss they were feeling, and my heart ached. His sentence was not long enough in my book, but the outcome allowed us to begin another healing process.

⁓

About six weeks after we came through this situation, I had a regular gynecologic check-up. I loved my doctor; he delivered all three of my kids, and he was kind, caring, and authentic. In fact, at the previous year's visit just three months after the tragedy, he came into the exam room and said, "Hi Cathy! How's it going? Are you getting any?"

That was his stock joke. I tried to laugh but couldn't. Instead, I looked at him and said, "Well, that would be a little hard since Dave was killed in a car accident three months ago."

"Oh, f**k!" he exclaimed. "I'm so sorry. I had no idea!"

There was nothing I could say except, "It's okay. Thank you."

He told me gently and honestly that I needed to give myself a little time, but that I shouldn't turn away from finding love again. "Everybody needs to be loved," he said. "Having sex is just part of that."

I was nowhere near ready to hear that, but I always appreciated him for being so candid as to say it. These days, every once in awhile, he still asks me the same question. Now I just smile.

On this particular visit, six weeks after Jennifer and I had gone court, the doctor suggested that I get a mammogram. I explained that I really hated the procedure, but he assured me that it was all routine, and it should be done. So I made the appointment for the week before Thanksgiving.

There was no getting around it. The procedure was not pleasant, especially when the technician came back in and took two more rounds of pictures. I wanted to cry. As I dressed and came out of the room, I was told to go into another room so a doctor could talk with me. I did as I was asked, and when he came in, he explained that he had read the films, and there was something on my right breast that needed to be attended to right away because it might be cancerous.

"What?" I snapped. "Are you kidding me? You're not even my doctor, and you have no bedside manner whatsoever, and you think it's okay to scare the crap out of me by being blunt?" I couldn't handle it.

The technician came back to talk to me. She said, "It's best if you call your doctor's office right away to get a follow-up appointment with him. He can explain everything."

My mind raced. *Breast cancer?* How would I take care of the kids? Would God really put me through having to say goodbye to my kids now, so soon after they lost their dad?

I did the only thing I could do at that moment: I prayed. And by the time I got home and called the doctor's office, I felt a little calmer. My appointment was booked for the following week, and

I asked God to help me keep this secret until I knew something definite.

By the time my appointment came around, I was a wreck. My doctor, whom I trusted, referred me to a breast surgeon who was working in his practice. My fear meter rose even more because I didn't know this person. I sat in her office and listened as she said, "Cathy, we need to do a biopsy to see what's going on."

"What does that mean?" I asked, trying not to let her see how I was shaking.

"It means we're going to put you under and go into the area of your breast that shows something out of the ordinary. We'll take a look and find out what's going on."

As she talked, my fear meter continued to rise. She asked, "Do you have any questions?"

I blurted out all my racing thoughts. "How likely is it that I have breast cancer? What are my chances of survival?" I didn't give her any time to answer. "What's my recovery time look like? How am I going to care for my kids? I don't have any family here."

She said gently, "Let's take things one step at a time. We'll get you scheduled for the biopsy, and then we'll go from there." She patted my hand and left the office.

An eternity passed as I waited. I think I cried as I prayed. "Lord, this sounds like a really big deal. Please don't let it be a big deal. Please give me the strength to handle whatever comes my way."

The surgery was scheduled for two weeks later because of the Thanksgiving holiday. I didn't want to tell anyone what was going on, but that night I went to my small group at church and broke down; it was a safe place, and I needed prayers, love, and support to get through this. Chris and Alicia listened and prayed with me, and even though I didn't want them to, they called my mom. Not because she could fly out and be with me, but so she would know about it. I was flying to a family event two days after the surgery, and Chris and

Alicia persuaded me that whatever happened, my mom should know what I'd been through before I got to the event.

As it all turned out, the lump was a calcification, and no further action was required. I was deeply thankful. It should have been a wakeup call for me to pay more attention to myself, but it wasn't. I quietly slipped back into my life of taking care of everyone else and staying as busy as I possibly could.

Big Leap

Therefore I say to you, do not worry about your life,
what you will eat or what you will drink; nor about
your body, what you will put on. Is not life more than food and the
body more than clothing? Look at the birds of the air,
for they neither sow nor reap nor gather into barns;
yet your heavenly Father feeds them.
Are you not of more value than they?
Matthew 6:25-26

I couldn't seem to find change on my own. Instead, change found me.

It all started when we visited Jennifer for a family weekend during her first year of college. I noticed this beautiful old home three blocks from her North Carolina campus that had been turned into apartments for college students, and that it was for sale. We had been told the college didn't have enough housing for upper-classmen, so I thought it might be good to purchase it, let Jennifer manage it, and ensure she had a place to live. What a great idea!

I got home from that weekend and called my accountant for advice. "What do you think about me buying real estate?" I told him about the housing situation and the building for sale.

"The real estate market has started to come back, so check it out," he said.

He told me about the changes happening in the housing market. While he was talking, I skimmed through my email. A subject line jumped out at me: "Lower Bucks Chamber Business for Sale." I was quite active in the chamber, and my immediate reaction was, "Who's selling their business, and I don't know about it?"

I opened the email to find it was from a member broker who was just putting out a listing of their businesses for sale. I scrolled through the listing until I came to one that said Newtown Day Spa.

My accountant was still talking. I interrupted him. "Hey, John," I said. "What do you think of me buying a spa in Newtown?"

He must have wondered what was going on in my head, but he didn't ask questions. Instead, he laughed. "It's as plausible as buying real estate in North Carolina," he said. "Check it out and see what you think."

That's exactly what I did. I called on both opportunities, and the broker set up a meeting with me two days later. The real estate agent in charge of the North Carolina property never returned my call, and to this day, I'm grateful that he didn't because when I saw the Newtown spa, I fell in love. For a long time afterward, my accountant and I joked about what a good thing it was that I didn't take my checkbook to that initial meeting. I'd have forked out anything the broker asked!

When I purchased Inner Spa, I bought it to have a business of my own, and because I enjoyed being pampered when I visited spas from time to time. I knew absolutely nothing about running a spa, but I thought I knew enough about business that I could run anything. I assembled an advisory team of eight individuals I knew and trusted: my accountant, personal banker, insurance agent, marketing consultant, graphic & web designer, lawyer, business coach, and a friend in a small business. Each of these individuals brought knowledge and insights into the process that I needed to ensure success.

During my due diligence process, we reviewed many documents and projected what might happen in three, five, and seven years based on the current numbers. I fielded questions about the business and how I would handle certain things, all of which made me better prepared to be the new owner. However, while I listened to the questions, I began to wonder about the viability of the signature service, colon hydrotherapy.

I'll never forget the day I was in a meeting with the bank and my business coach, who was also my acquisition manager. Someone asked, "How are you going to make money from cleaning poop?"

Cleaning poop. Apparently, that was colon hydrotherapy in a nutshell, and suddenly, it didn't sound so fantastic. "Well," I said, trying to sound more confident than I felt, "as you can see from the numbers, the current owner is doing very well. I'm sure I'll be able to continue the trends and make a healthy profit going forward."

Inside, though, I was questioning myself. What was I doing? How was I going to make money from colon hydrotherapy, this service that, let's face it, I knew nothing about? I started to question my decision to buy this business, so I called my coach.

"Do I have to keep everything just the way it is once I buy the business?" I asked.

"No," she said. "Once you sign the papers, it's yours to do with as you please."

"Okay, so I can get rid of colon hydrotherapy if I want to." It was a statement, not a question.

She said. "Yes, if that's what you want to do."

A game plan formed in my mind as we moved forward with the last few weeks of due diligence. We lined up the financing, designed a new logo, and got projections in place; you might say I got my ducks in a row. Then, about two weeks before closing, a small voice told me I needed to learn more about colon hydrotherapy.

Hmmm. If I got rid of that service, would I really be doing the right thing?

The nudge was strong enough to make me pick up the phone and call the owner. "Hi, Sharon. I think I need to learn more about colon hydrotherapy."

"Of course," she said. "I'll teach you as part of the business transition."

That wasn't all I wanted, though. Sharon had talked about a certification process, and I found myself thinking maybe I should do that. "No," I said. "Can you tell me more about what it takes to get certified in that kind of therapy?"

She sounded surprised. After all, even if I kept the service, I certainly didn't have to perform it myself. "Well, sure," she said, "but why?"

"I want to be able to talk about it, credibly," I told her. "I'd like to understand what it does so that when I explain it, people take me seriously."

She understood and laid out what I needed to do. That afternoon, I got started with an approved online A&P course. I chuckle when I think about that because it just goes to show that God does have a sense of humor. When I was in school, I hated science, even though I got good grades in every course I took. I graduated with a B.A. in English and business rather than a B.S., and I never thought I would do anything that resembled being in the healthcare field. Yet here I was, taking an A&P course and learning about the human body to buy a holistic day spa.

❧

I do believe that God led me to buy this particular business, and I kept exercising my trust throughout the entire purchasing process. I didn't know exactly why I needed this business, though, until quite some time after the purchase was complete.

The day after signing the papers, I began learning the business. Two things became quite clear to me that first day: 1) I needed to learn as much as I could about holistic living, and 2) I needed to stop drinking soda, Diet Coke in particular. The first would be challenging but fun; I've always enjoyed learning something new. The second... well, that's a bit of a story.

I grew up in what was once the Coca-Cola capital of the world. Wenona, Illinois, sold more Coca-Cola per capita than any other city or town anywhere. I grew up drinking diet vanilla marshmallow cokes and loved them. When I moved to Pennsylvania in my mid-twenties, I bought Diet Coke by the case. By the time I bought the Spa, I was consuming upwards of sixty ounces of Diet Coke per day. As soon as I found out what it did to my body...yikes!

When I learned how badly soda—not just Diet Coke, but all soda—affected my digestive system and relaxation (after all, I was new in the digestive and relaxation business), I made the decision to stop cold turkey. That part turned out to be easier than I'd expected. The bigger challenge, as it happened, was switching to water as my beverage of choice. That actually took longer to achieve than giving up soda.

I didn't realize it at the time, but giving up soda and changing to water were two important steps on my path to self-care. Baby steps, for sure, but important baby steps that helped to form a foundation on which I could build. If I hadn't bought my new business, I don't know if I ever would have taken those first tiny steps.

When we do things that aid the body, it can function at its best, and support the lifestyle we desire and deserve to live. Our bodies won't let us down unless we don't take care of them the way they need. That's why self-care is so important, especially in today's world.

Self-care has many aspects. It's a dynamic concept for most people because what "self-care" means for anyone can change over time. For most of my life, I hated exercise. I loved to be active, but organized exercise classes just were not my cup of tea. Going for a walk or hiking or playing ball or swimming were more my speed, and I was okay with not having a regular exercise routine. However, as I continued to learn more about holistic living, I began to realize that regular exercise and movement were important to the mind/body/spirit connection.

My new business got me to learn more about exercise and how important it really was for whole living, but it still took me a long while before I truly embraced it as an important part of my wellness journey. I talked about it with clients but never felt comfortable guiding them, because I didn't do the same work for myself. I needed to learn how to walk the talk, but that was far from easy.

Addictions

Not only so, but we also glory in our sufferings,
because we know that suffering produces
perseverance; perseverance, character;
and character, hope. And hope does not put us to shame,
because God's love has been poured out into our
hearts through the Holy Spirit, who has been
given to us.
Romans 5:3-5

I love my oldest son, just as I love each of my children, but I must admit that my relationship with Bryan has always been strained. He has given me a run for my money when it comes to following the rules and doing the right thing. There have been many arguments, raised voices, hurt feelings, and heartbreaking times over the years. I didn't want to make excuses for him, I just wanted him to be the best version of himself he could be.

About seven months after purchasing the spa, and just a few weeks after Bryan's sixteenth birthday, I traveled to England with my friend Sharon. Although I had made arrangements for another friend to stay with the boys, that's when my troubles with Bryan escalated as he was arrested and put in juvenile detention the night I returned from that trip. What an ending to a trip that was otherwise wonderful!

That was Bryan's first encounter with the law. He was put in a juvenile placement facility in December 2011, just before Christmas. For the next nine months, I would drive twenty-three and a half miles each way every Wednesday to visit my son. And when he was granted weekend days, I would drive up and back twice in a day just so he could be with his family, spend time with us, and so he would know how much we loved him. Yes, my car knew the way quite well.

Life was anything but normal at this point, but I kept plodding, doing the best I could. My health suffered, even though I didn't recognize it at the time. I pushed a lot of emotional stress aside because it was too painful to deal with. Questions bubbled in my head: Was I the cause of Bryan's choices? Was it the death of his father? Had Bryan been left with the "wrong" parent to take care of him? The mind games were powerful - I tried to be tougher. I told myself I could handle everything on my own, and then I pushed my pain aside, trying to focus on my son and whatever I could do to make things right for him.

Bryan came home just in time to start school the next fall. For a while, things seemed to be better; at least, Bryan and I argued less. Then, on October 29, 2012, Hurricane Sandy hit our area. It was Bryan's seventeenth birthday. He and I went out in the morning to survey the damage in our yard and neighborhood, and when I saw how he was acting, I realized he was high. When I confronted him about it, he also admitted that at night after I went to bed, he would sneak out of the house alone. He refused to tell me anything about what he did during those nights.

I was devastated; in fact, heartbroken. Bryan had already put himself in danger and spent time in the legal system, at no small hurt and pain and inconvenience to me. I felt like I could look ahead and see endless trouble for him and for us, his family. What was it going to take to get him to change his behavior? When was enough going to be enough?

I had no idea how to deal with my teenage son, no idea how to reach him and get him back on the right track. I didn't know anyone who had been through something like this. Worse, I didn't want anyone to know I had a son who was making bad choices (that's what I called it at that time because it made it all a little easier to handle). I didn't want anyone to judge me as a "bad parent" and assume that I was the reason behind his choices. And yes, I did wrestle with the idea that it was somehow my fault.

I think, as parents, we have the best of intentions. We want our children to "have it better than we did." Sometimes that's too much parental strain to put on ourselves. I had a very good childhood: parents who loved me, family to surround me and support me, teachers who saw leadership and possibilities in me and made sure I had the opportunity to explore them all. My children had parents who loved them, a family who surrounded them and supported them. And yes, they had teachers who saw good in them and tried to steer them in a positive direction. Bryan just didn't always understand that.

Because of the mind games going on inside my head, I tried to overcompensate and make everything okay for him. I didn't want him to get in trouble; I just wanted him to feel all right, to be all right. I made excuses and rationalized his behavior. Now I understand that I enabled him through my actions, or rather, through not holding him accountable for his own actions.

After Hurricane Sandy, I briefly tried to be firm with Bryan. I told him that I wouldn't put up with his shenanigans and that he had to follow the rules. That lasted about two minutes. I simply didn't have the resilience or determination to enforce what I'd said. My level of emotional stress was too high, so I tried—again—to push what I felt aside, and tell myself things were getting better, Bryan was going to be fine. I didn't sleep much over the next weeks, because I would stay up to make sure he didn't sneak out. When I did fall asleep, it was fitful at best.

I remember one morning, arguing with him about some particular responsibility he'd sluffed off.

He yelled. "I can't wait until I'm eighteen, and I can move out of this house! I'll do better on my own!"

Ouch! I felt so hurt. I don't know what I'd expected him to say, but it wasn't that. Here was my little boy, hurting and needing love, and he just wanted to get away from me.

Then, in January of 2013, things really escalated with Bryan. He snuck out of the house one Monday night and never came home.

As any parent would, I went into a panic. Bryan had long since stopped bringing friends to the house, so I didn't have any idea who he might be with. I called everyone I could think of. I drove around the neighborhood, looking down driveways and in backyards. I stopped by one home at the end of our street, where a friend's grandmother lived. No, she hadn't seen him.

Bryan was on probation at that point, so I had to call the police. I had to tell them my son had violated the terms of that probation by removing himself from my supervision and effectively disappearing. No mother wants to report her own child to the police, but at that point, I only wanted Bryan found and safe. The officers said they would look for him.

While I waited, I went into Bryan's room. Something led me to start looking around; I must have been hunting for any clues I could find, anywhere. Behind a wall poster, I found a stash of weed. I couldn't help thinking that was a clever hiding place. Then I found a journal, sitting out in plain sight. Before I knew it, I found myself reading Bryan's own testimony about his addictions to heroin and cocaine.

I couldn't believe those words on the page, in the handwriting I knew so well. As I sat there, dumbfounded, my phone rang. It was the mother of a friend of Bryan's, who told me that she believed

Bryan was hiding in a playhouse in her backyard. I thanked her and called the police again. I had to give them that lead. Several hours later, the phone rang again; it was Bryan, telling me that he had been arrested and would be taken back to juvenile detention shortly.

Talk about heartbreak. On the one hand, I was elated that he was safe. On the other hand, he was going to be locked up again, and I didn't know how he—or I—could bear that. And on top of that, I was devastated by what I had learned that day about his drug use. It was all too much to handle. I still thank God that I never once tried to drown my troubles by drinking, or self-medicating, or anything like that. I just kept pushing my pain aside and ate to drown my feelings.

All of this happened the week of my birthday. You can imagine that I didn't feel much like celebrating, but my daughter convinced me to drive down and visit her for a long weekend. A.J. and I drove down to North Carolina and had a good weekend, visiting the beautiful Biltmore Estate in Asheville on a fine, chilly day. During that trip, it hit me forcibly that I had two other children who needed and deserved just as much of my attention as Bryan had been receiving. He had gotten so much of my time and energy over the previous two years that I hadn't really spent much quality time with Jennifer and A.J. I asked myself, *What am I doing?*

That weekend, I vowed that I would make changes in the way I parented Bryan. I would still be his mother. I would still love him. But I would have to be honest about who he was and what he was doing. I would have to face the difficulties head-on and not make excuses for him anymore.

When I got home from my trip, I asked for prayers for Bryan. I told my small group candidly about what he had been doing and what I'd found out about his drug use. It was almost a relief when I did, because I learned that drugs have affected so many people's lives. I found that I had a community who would be there for me, listen non-judgmentally, pray, and pray some more. I also began to learn that the opioid epidemic in our community was rising to an all-time high. No one was entirely safe from it. The more I learned, the more people shared their stories with me and told me how they'd come through experiences like mine. I was floored but also encouraged. I was not alone.

Bryan came home four months later. From the start, he talked a good game about how he had changed. He got a job and seemed more engaged in our family. But it was all smoke and mirrors, as I found out when I returned from a convention in Florida that June.

I had a wonderful time at the convention. It refueled my passion for my work, and I was eager to get home and apply what I'd learned during those five days. My business had suffered during the time that I'd been handling Bryan, so I was excited to get back to work. But the night I got home from Florida, Bryan came in from work, and right away I saw that he was acting strange. At first, he didn't even speak to me. When he did, he didn't seem like himself.

He finally asked how my trip was. I told him it had been great, and couldn't help sharing that I'd even won an award. "Colon hydrotherapist of the year," I said, smiling. "How about that?"

He barely seemed to hear me. "That's nice," he said. I guess he noticed that I wanted more because he added, "Work's okay, but I'm really tired."

Part of me thought I should leave it alone, but his behavior was really worrying me. "Why are you so tired?" I asked. "What were you doing while I was away?"

I was afraid to ask the question: afraid of what he might say or not say, afraid to burst the bubble of happiness I'd brought back from the convention. I was right to be scared.

"Lay off, Mom!" he snapped. "I'm tired because I've been working hard."

That wasn't the end of it. He ranted at me, his face and voice distorted with anger. All I could get was that anger; what he said didn't make much sense. I tried not to notice the fear and sadness that started to swallow me.

When he finally paused, I tried to calm things down. "Why don't you go up to bed and get some sleep," I suggested. "We can talk in the morning."

"I don't want to talk. Stop trying to control me," he yelled.

I couldn't tolerate that disrespect, and our discussion turned into an argument, with both of us throwing angry words at each other. Finally, he shouted at me to leave him the hell alone. As he stormed away up the stairs, I heard him add, "I don't have to listen to you!"

That was when I lost it. I followed him upstairs and stood in the doorway of his room. "I am still your mother." I forced my voice to remain calm, praying I could keep myself from shouting. "You do have to listen to me. You cannot make these bad choices that take you to places that are not good for you."

He swung around with his fist raised. Before I knew it, he was coming at me. When I stepped aside, his fist connected with the door. What a sound! What a hole!

I knew at that moment I couldn't do anything for him. "I'm not going to talk with you when you're like this," I said. I turned away and headed downstairs.

Bryan was taken back to juvenile detention for a third time at the end of July. At that point, I started asking some different questions.

Up until then, I had been praying that God would open Bryan's eyes to the lessons he needed to learn. I had prayed that God would help him to make good decisions. Now, I started asking God why Bryan wasn't learning the lessons he needed to.

At about the same time, our pastor began a sermon series about prayer and listening for answers. One of the messages centered around praying for something to change, yet finding yourself in the same situation over and over again. The pastor said if that happens, maybe it's because we need to learn something we haven't realized yet.

As Bryan was put in his third placement, this time, a juvenile boot camp about four hours from home, I started looking at the situations I kept finding myself in with him. I changed the question. What did I need to learn? He kept making bad choices, and despite my own best intentions, I kept making excuses. Through much prayer and talking with friends, I began to realize that I needed to learn to let go and realize I couldn't control all the outcomes anymore. Bryan was old enough to make his own decisions. I had to let him do it. It didn't mean I didn't love him or want the best for him; it simply meant that I needed to let the chips fall where they might so that he had to deal with the consequences of his own actions. It's very hard to do that when you feel like you're watching your child self-destruct.

Slowly, very slowly, I began to adopt a new attitude toward Bryan. Because he was so far away this time, I couldn't go and visit him except for a couple of times during the four months he was in this program. He turned eighteen while there, but I could only send him a card because it wasn't his visitation weekend.

Meanwhile, I did all I could to detach myself from his drama and focus on my other children and my business. Left on his own, Bryan began to make progress. I was very proud when I went up that December for his graduation from the program and saw the accolades he'd received. I felt hopeful that, this time, he'd made real changes, although in the back of my mind, I was scared of what would happen to us if he hadn't. Time would tell.

~

As fate would have it, my hopefulness was short-lived. Six weeks later, on January 31, 2014, I woke up at 5:30 in the morning to the phone ringing. When I picked up, I heard Bryan crying on the other end.

"I'm sorry, Mom. I'm really sorry. I didn't mean it. I'm really sorry, Mommy. Can you help me? Please?"

Parents reading this, I hope you never get a phone call like that. One minute I was fast asleep. The next minute, I was trying to figure out what my son was doing on the phone when he should have been upstairs in his bed. When I was finally able to understand what he was talking about, I realized that he had been arrested for breaking and entering.

At first, he tried to make it sound like a harmless prank. I soon learned that it was much more serious than that, and he was now, legally, an adult.

Remember how I was working on me? That all went straight to hell in a handbasket. As it turned out, a member of my care team, Beverley, was scheduled to be at my house that day to do some work for our professional organization, the International Association for Colon Hydrotherapy (I-ACT). God certainly does have a way of putting angels exactly where we need them. She listened to me. Cried with me. She held my hand and comforted me. I still couldn't believe what was happening, but by the end of the weekend, my mind had cleared a little.

This began a new chapter in my relationship with Bryan. As an adult, he was charged and put in the county jail. There, he got clean and put his mind to doing all the work necessary to complete his senior year on time. He got counseling. By the time he went before the judge again in May, he seemed to be on the right track. The judge must have thought so too because he let Bryan go into the work-release program, and signed off on him getting out to begin college in August.

Self-Examination

But test everything; hold fast what is good.
1 Thessalonians 5:21

That spring, Jennifer got engaged. It was a happy time, even though our family was fractured. We began talking about wedding plans, which was fun; it was a distraction from the troubles with Bryan.

In May, we traveled to Charlotte for Jennifer's graduation: my parents, my friends Chris and Rich, my brother and sister-in-law, A.J., and me. All of us were there to celebrate Jennifer's accomplishments, except for Bryan.

Just before he was to be released, Bryan made another choice, which now meant that he had to serve weekends, but could get out to attend classes at the community college. I couldn't help despairing again. Would he ever learn? Would I ever learn how to deal with him? My life once again focused on him, because I had to take him to and from the county jail every weekend, so he could be incarcerated for those forty-eight hours.

The first weekend in October, I had to be in Tennessee for a board meeting. A fellow board member and one of my care team, Tiffany, came home with me for a visit. I went to pick up Bryan that Sunday evening, and he was not where he was supposed to be. No one could really help me other than to say he was back at the jail. It took me nearly a week to find out what had happened. The long and short of it was he had a hot urine test when he went in on Friday, which meant that the test showed evidence of drug use. He had violated the terms of his release and would have to serve the rest of his sentence in full.

No more college that semester. At that point, the money aspect of the situation began to set in for me. I had spent a small fortune on my son in the past four years, money that would never be recouped. Emotional stress, lack of sleep, time away from my business, and now the realization that financial stress could be an issue crushed me. How much more could I take? Would things ever get better?

Bryan was released to a halfway house in March 2015. The house was not far from our home, so we saw him periodically. He got a job and eventually found a room to rent. He attended meetings and often spoke of learning to live in recovery and staying clean. Things seemed to be going better for Bryan this time. And I felt very comfortable with my decision that he could not live under my roof again. I loved him, but I couldn't have him pull me down again.

As I have said, self-care is not a "one size fits all" proposition. In fact, self-care might be totally different for you than it is for me. What is important to totally understand is this: self-care begins and ends with you. Self-care is all about the relationship you have with yourself—your mind, body, and spirit.

Since embarking on the latest iteration of my wellness journey (thirty-one months as of this writing), I have had to look at what the mind/body/spirit connection means to me. More importantly, I've had to look at what self-care means to the healthy balance of my mind/body/spirit connection.

Lately, I've often been asked, "What does that mean, and why is it so important to my self-care and well-being?" Good questions. First, let's look at what the mind/body/spirit connection means.

Every human being has a core. At the core are the mind (our

emotions), the spirit (our relationship to something bigger than our-selves—in my case, my faith), and the body (our physical being). These three sides of human existence need to be in balance—in harmony if you will—for the body to function optimally.

Think of it as a triangle, with each side being one element of the core. For the triangle to stay balanced, each side has to hold its weight to support the other two sides. When the balance is main-tained—when harmony exists in the body—the core is happy. When an imbalance exists in one or more sides, the body tries to compen-sate for what is missing, and all hell breaks loose.

That is what happened in my life. I did not want anyone to know that I was less than totally together, so I worked really hard at hiding myself behind a mask. I got so good at it (or so I told myself I did) that I forgot about the emotional side of the equation for many years. I was a widow, the mother of three, a business owner, and a darn good certified colon hydrotherapist. What did I need with emotional entanglements anyway? And so, I lived for quite some time without balance in my life. Unfortunately, without balance, nothing in my life was really right.

I would like to take some time now to explore the "mind" leg of the triangle with you. No one ever explained these concepts to me in a way I truly understood, so I hope that by explaining it here, I will make your wellness journey a little easier, a little more attainable.

The mind is a terrible thing to waste, but it is also where we have to choose positivity or negativity. Our thoughts play a big part in our overall self-care because the more positive your thoughts, the more positive your outlook on life. We all need to spend time with our thoughts. If you don't, you really should: I know because I ran from mine for years without ever realizing what I was doing. Because of that, you should only entertain good, healthy, encouraging, and uplifting thoughts.

Have you ever heard the expression "your mind is playing tricks on you"? Well, it is more than an expression. When you spend time in negative thoughts, your mind is taking you down a path that is no trick, and if you are not careful, you will find you have gone so far you cannot come back. When negativity sets in, ask yourself, "Is this where I want to live my life?" If the answer is "no" then run in the opposite direction! Make the conscious decision to find the positive in the situation and turn things back to the right path.

The mind is more than just positive vs. negative. Although that has a lot to do with keeping the mind healthy, it is also about emotional well-being. I will admit, this was the hardest for me to understand, but understanding your emotional side is just as important—if not more so—than the physical and spiritual sides of the triangle. If your emotions are not open, if they are not dealt with positively, they will keep you blocked without you ever knowing what is happening. Like many things in life, emotional blockage happens over time. The only way I know to change it is to face it head-on because you cannot go around it, under it or over it. You simply have to come through it to get to the other side.

For nearly eleven years, I never saw the change in my emotional well-being. I had always been a happy person, outgoing and genuine. I smiled a lot and enjoyed life, which wasn't a bed of roses, but I was happy. When the rug was pulled out from my world, I slowly, *oh so slowly*, slipped into the abyss now known as the 'old Cathy.' Little by little, I lost my happiness but did everything I could to not let people know. Little by little, my smile and brightness faded. Even though I erected a façade, I secretly did not like life. I didn't want to get out and participate unless I had to.

I could feel something was not right, and I felt powerless to change it, as I had no idea where to begin or who to turn to. I continued to focus on everything under the sun but me, and in the process, I pushed people aside. Why? Because I knew what was best for me and did not need anyone else to tell me what I needed. I guess you could say I became a real bitch, and for a long time, I did not really care.

How did I keep going? As I look back, I think I tried really hard to royally screw up my life. Once again, I believe God had a plan, a purpose to prosper me. He used every situation I found myself in to help me through the emotional fog I walked in for so long.

~

My wake-up call came when A.J.—who now went by his full name, Andrew—was accepted to college five and half years after I bought the Spa. By then, Jennifer was married, Bryan was doing his thing, and I only had one child left at home.

It shocked me at the beginning of that school year to take Andrew's picture on the first day, the way I'd always done. He had grown up without me realizing it. Almost six feet tall, with facial hair: he wasn't a boy anymore, but a young man. How had that happened? And he didn't even need me to drive him to school anymore; he was driving himself, had a parking permit at school, and was so excited at his newfound independence that I had to be happy for him, but I couldn't believe he didn't need Mom to drop him off anymore.

In early October, Andrew came home from school one day, very excited about going on a visit to the Penn College of Technology, the same college his favorite teacher had attended. Andrew wanted to go to the open house at the end of the month, so we registered and made plans.

The Penn College, in Williamsport, is three hours from where we live, so we drove up on Saturday evening as things started early on Sunday. We got registered just before the tour began.

The campus was small and beautiful, with lots of personality. Our student tour guide told us about the history of the college, the different technical areas offered, and campus life. I chuckled at the fact that my late husband was a big University of Illinois fan, and our youngest son only wanted to attend a Penn State-affiliated school. But then, knowing how much Dave valued education, I realized he would have been just as pleased as I was that Andrew was so excited about pursuing his degree.

"So, what do you think, A.J.?" I asked when the tour was over.

"Well, I like it. It's small and easy to get around, and I'm not far from home. Not that I'll be coming home every weekend," he said, grinning.

I was glad he liked the visit—I had really enjoyed having these couple of days with him—but in the back of my mind, I was trying not to think about what his absence from home would mean. How empty the house would feel.

He sent in an online application as soon as we got back home. Then he announced that he didn't want to visit any other colleges because Penn College was, hands down, the only school he wanted. I was proud I'd raised a son who knew his mind and had confidence in his choices.

The acceptance letter came the weekend after Thanksgiving. Andrew and I had just gotten home from a visit to Jennifer and her husband in North Carolina, where my parents had joined us. Andrew opened the mail and immediately shared the news. "Mom! I got in!"

I was so excited for him and proud of him, but when he ran upstairs to call some friends, I sat at the breakfast bar with a rapidly-cooling mug of tea and cried silently in sheer terror. The news of my son's imminent departure for college was real, and I felt completely undone. My breathing sped up, my head began to spin, and I heard ringing in my ears. I couldn't have moved if my life had depended on it at that moment.

I remember thinking, "Holy shit! I'm going to be alone in this big house, and I'm going to have to spend time with somebody I really don't like."

That was the exact truth. I was going to be alone for the first time in thirty-five years. That meant I was going to have to spend an awful lot of time with myself, and I did not especially like me.

Realizing how I felt about myself came hard. I had spent

countless hours learning about holistic living and detoxification. I had worked with clients to help them on their wellness journeys, and I knew intellectually that something needed to change for me. Even though I had the tools at my disposal and the knowledge to make changes, I had absolutely no idea where to begin. It would be some time yet before I found the right first steps.

Into the New Year

*I lift up my eyes to the mountains—where does my help come from?
My help comes from the Lord, the Maker of heaven and earth. The Lord
watches over you. The Lord will keep you from all harm—he will watch
over your life; the Lord will watch over your coming and going both
now and forevermore.*

Psalm 121

By the time Andrew's college acceptance came, Christmas was just a few short weeks away. I wrote down a few thoughts and promised myself I would look into it right after the new year. Yes, I had made myself similar promises in the past, but this time I knew it had to be different. This time, the promise stayed in my thoughts all the time.

Christmas has always been a special time of year for me, in large part because of my faith and being surrounded by family. When Dave was alive, we always had a large Douglas Fir tree that the whole family decorated with tons of ornaments. We decorated the house, sent out lots of cards with a family letter, and had at least one holiday party. The house was always a festive place filled with love and laughter.

Christmas morning was always filled with anticipation. I don't know who was more excited, Dave or the kids. Stockings hung in the hallway along the stairs, and the kids would empty them with such excitement while Daddy took pictures and looked on. While I made coffee, tea, and hot chocolate, and got the breakfast casserole and cinnamon rolls in the oven, one of the kids would get a large garbage bag, and Dave would light the fireplace and turn on the Christmas music. Then we would settle in and open presents. Dave insisted that each person get a couple of presents before everyone opened their gifts one at a time. Yes, Christmas was filled with lots of love and tradition.

After the accident, I still held Christmas as a special time, but things changed, evolved really. We changed the decorations to fit the home improvements and the openness of the house. Instead of a letter, I created a photo page to show the kids throughout the year. Giving presents took on a new meaning as we began participating in the Angel Tree, a program that helps ensure children in need have gifts to open on Christmas morning. We also adopted a family in need, giving gifts and food. We still hosted our annual Christmas party, but we were more intentional about spending time with family and friends, and doing holiday activities that brought meaning to the season.

Christmas of 2016 was one of the best since losing Dave. Andrew helped me with some of the decorations, but I had started the most wonderful decorating concept the previous year: I hired someone to come in and help me! It was truly a wonderful self-care practice, even though I didn't realize that's what it was when I started.

My parents didn't join us that year, but all of my kids— Jennifer and her husband Dustin, Bryan and Andrew—were home, and we had a wonderful time together. It was the first time in many years that everyone was smiling, laughing, and getting along really well. We had a photo taken. Although I don't really like the way I look in that photo, because I wasn't physically in shape, I will always cherish the memory because it was a new chapter. I just didn't know what that meant at the time.

~

After the holidays, the house felt empty without the laughter of the kids being home. Jennifer and Dustin went back to their lives in North Carolina, Bryan was working (not living at home), and Andrew was back to school. Even the kitties were quiet.

Bryan had asked me to help him get an apartment, so we spent some time together looking for a place early in the new year. I always wanted my time with Bryan to be special and filled with joy, but our relationship had been pretty strained to that point, so it always seemed harder than it needed to be. I couldn't shake the heaviness in my heart; I was worried he would make unwise choices again without my constant guidance. While my head understood that I had to let him make his way in the world and figure out life on his own terms, my heart found it really hard to do, because he was still my little boy.

He found a place that was a five-minute drive from the house, and Andrew and I helped him move in on my birthday that January. I hadn't wanted to celebrate my birthday for several years, but when we finished setting up Bryan's place, the boys and I went out to dinner. Although we had a nice time, I knew I wasn't really living. I sat at the table listening to the boys talk about computer games or something, and I wanted my life to be different. I wanted to trust my son, but I found that to be a difficult task. I wanted to be happy, but I didn't know what that meant. As I thought about all these things, Bryan broke through the chatter in my head.

"Thank you for all your help, Mom," he said. "I really appreciate you helping me find the place and getting it set up. You too, A.J."

"You're welcome," I said, managing to smile.

Bryan said, "Happy birthday, Mom. I'm sorry I don't have a birthday present for you, but I promise I'll do right this time."

I thought about all that had gone before with my son. I just wanted him to be the best version of himself he could be, but I also knew I couldn't do it for him. "Just make good choices," I said. "Be all you were created to be, and that will be the best birthday present you can give me."

I'm not sure why that memory is as vivid as it is, but I think my emotionally closed-off existence was catching up to me. I was tired of looking over my shoulder, wondering when the other shoe would drop with my son. I was tired of feeling like I wasn't living. I was tired, just plain tired, of feeling so empty yet trying to show the world I was strong and doing fine.

~

True to my promise to myself, I began the arduous process of looking at my deep-rooted fear that January of 2017, searching several areas of my life to figure out where it came from. I had a good and loving upbringing and a family who supported me always, so I did not think it went back that far. I had a good marriage with mutual love and respect, but that had been taken away from me unexpectedly. Hmmm...that was something to consider.

I was very fortunate to receive many wonderful opportunities in my early career, and I became very focused on my professional success at a young age. I had always worked hard and long hours... maybe there was something there.

I was the best mother I could be, the best father I could imagine. Once my children were all out of the house, who would I be then? Was that where the fear came from?

I had not been alone—really alone—since my first apartment in college, and then I only lived alone for about six months before changing apartments and getting a roommate. From there, I got married and had kids. Was I afraid to be alone again?

My head was spinning as I began to look at all of these things. It was too much to consider all at once. I decided I needed to figure out who I was.

Was I the widowed mother of three kids? Was I the business-woman who was trying to thrive, or the marketer who was always creating? Was I a spiritual person, a good friend? Was I a judgmental bitch on wheels, or was I an encourager? Who was I, and more importantly, who did I want to be?

These were not easy questions. When I first tried to answer them, writing down the first things that came to mind, I was less than honest with myself. As I sat there staring at the words on the page, a little voice said: "Answer them again, but this time look deeper for the truth."

What? I was truthful, wasn't I? My first instinct was to chuck the whole exercise, but I didn't. Instead, I set it aside for a while and focused on a long weekend trip to San Diego with two girlfriends.

I wish I could tell you how much time I spent looking at where my fear came from, but I can't. There were days I felt as though I was thinking about it constantly, other days it seemed like it was just a few minutes. Every time I really tried to unpack the fear it was hard work because I had to look at myself and be honest about what I saw. I had to open doors, and I didn't want to see what was on the other side.

I think that's why hearing a voice say to "go deeper" sent me into a tizzy. I had never had to go any deeper than the surface to find answers, but then I had never been in this particular state before, so I was in uncharted territory. I had a restlessness at work and was just beginning to understand that I was not really walking the talk I was giving my clients. There was a congruency issue. How could I be a successful holistic practitioner if I didn't practice what I suggested others do? I didn't like who I had become, but I didn't know why I had become that way. I was tired of putting on a face for the world to see, yet feeling down and alone. I think the combination of all those things ultimately made me listen to the voice and want to go deeper. I just needed time.

My Care Team

Therefore, as God's chosen people, holy and dearly loved,
clothe yourselves with compassion, kindness,
humility, gentleness, and patience.
Colossians 3:12

First, though, the trip to San Diego. The last week in January 2017, was cool, sunny, and beautiful in Southern California. For five glorious days, I didn't have a care in the world. (Well, I did, but I ran away for a few days to hide from them...again!)

Two of the people I traveled with that weekend are part of my "care team," as I like to call them. Sharon, my traveling buddy, also owned a small business, and we attended the same church. She and I met in a networking group in 2003. We didn't immediately become fast friends, but over the years we developed a strong bond that stands the test of time. This time we traveled because we both needed to have some space from work, or as I put it at the time, we both needed to get out of dodge. We planned the long weekend in San Diego, where we met up with another friend, Tiffany, who lives in California.

I want to mention the other members of my care team: Beverley, Gail Marie, and Suzanne. Each of them has helped me challenge myself and grow in so many ways. I have so much in common with each of them both professionally and in our shared faith. While not all of them could be with Tiffany, Sharon, and me during the long weekend in California, they were an invaluable part of the journey I started on that trip.

Those five days with Sharon and Tiffany were a special time. Sharon was a matter of fact, no-nonsense. She was funny and caring, and she challenged me to think about things in ways I might not have considered before. Tiffany was the fun-loving one of the team; she liked to bring laughter into every situation. She had experienced things in her life that gave her a unique perspective, and she brought that to hold me accountable and move forward. As I thought about it, there was no coincidence that I spent that weekend in San Diego with these two women. Their presence, their friendship, their love were exactly what I needed at that time.

Since this journey began, I have had people ask me who I saw to work through emotional issues, and my simple answer is, "I didn't see anyone." That's right, I did not find a counselor and sit in their office every week to figure out what my fear was and why I had it. Instead, I had the blessing of five great women—friends, colleagues, sisters—who had been through various life events and training who were always—and I do mean always!—there for me. And they were not all around the corner from me. One lived about ten minutes away, one in Connecticut, one in Florida, one in Arizona, and one in California. These amazing women, along with my family and a few dear friends who have always prayed for, encouraged, and supported me, were my counselors. No matter what time, day or night, I could call or text them, and they were there for me, helping to figure out my fear and my life. They never said, "Oh, you'll be okay." Quite the opposite. They held me accountable and challenged me to think about my feelings, consider new ways of looking at things, and getting out of my comfort zone.

The trip to San Diego was wonderful in every way. I laughed and celebrated life like I had not done in a long time. Even though it was two and a half weeks after the fact, we celebrated my birthday; we went oystering and pulled pearls, which has now become a tradition with me, and I try to do it anytime I'm somewhere it can be done. I embraced being on the beach in Coronado, watching a beautiful sand sculpture being created, and thinking how nice it would be if life were simple and straightforward, just like that sculpture.

I didn't completely forget my problems, though. While my friends and I were at the San Diego Zoo one day, I caught myself thinking about my fear and the surface answers I had written to the questions I'd posed for myself back home. I thought about the fun I was having and how I was a little bit of a different person when I spent time 3,000 miles from my life. What was up with that?

I told my friends about my fears of being an empty-nester, how I soon wouldn't have any kids at home, and that I wasn't sure what to do with myself. Sharon and Tiffany commented that it would be nice to not have anyone else to worry about. (One of them had a son still living at home, and the other never had kids.)

I said, "I guess that would be nice—eventually. What do I do with all the time on my hands?"

We talked and brainstormed all kinds of things, silly and serious. Maybe I could do more with my business, or get more into essential oils, or crafting. Maybe I could do some consulting. Although I didn't find any answers that weekend, I had a lot to consider. The love and laughter my friends and I shared opened doors in my mind.

I returned from that weekend to find myself sick for the first time in five years. I couldn't believe it! I took my supplements. I ate healthy foods. I lived holistically, without chemicals in my house. Why was this happening to me? How could I spend five straight days on my couch, feeling like I was dying?

Slowly, I began to feel better. As I got back to myself, I heard a voice telling me, *Look at the foods you're eating.* At first, I didn't understand. Look at the foods I'm eating? What does that mean?

I heard the same message again and again until I finally walked into my kitchen one day to find something to eat. After five days of not wanting food, I was finally hungry. I picked up a box of oatmeal cookies, walked back to the living room, sat on the couch, and started eating. One, two, three cookies without blinking an eye. And then it hit me: *look at the foods you are eating!*

That was the start. Over the next couple of weeks, I tracked what I ate; I didn't change anything, just wrote everything down. I ate fresh veggies and lean proteins: yay me! But I ate cookies, chips, granola bars, dark chocolate, and "healthy" pre-packaged snacks, all without thinking about what I did or noticing the overall amounts I took in. I also noticed that I was eating the greens and lean proteins at work and when I was with others. Everything else—all the snacky, carby, comfort foods—I scarfed down at home, mostly when I was alone or when my youngest son was upstairs in his room. Wow! That was an eye-opener, for sure.

That was when I first realized I was an emotional eater; I ate without thinking about it. As I looked deeper, I also realized I ate when I was stressed, when I was tired, when I was sad or mad, and even when I was happy. And I was not eating healthily as I had been telling myself I was. Imagine my shock, real shock, because I'd truly believed I was eating well.

Food is critical: it's how we nourish our bodies, it's the fuel that makes us go. Yet I had never really paid attention to exactly what kinds of fuel I was putting in my body. Sure, I had fresh fruits and vegetables in my refrigerator, but I also had the processed, refined sugar-filled stuff in the house. As I began to unpack the fact that I was an emotional eater, I began to realize I had a choice to make. I could either make mindful food choices and make my life healthier, or I could continue eating what I had been and just tell myself I was healthy.

I have always tried to be honest and tell it like it is; I'm not in the habit of being hypocritical. Yet that's exactly what I was doing. The definition of emotional eating is the "propensity to eat in response to positive and negative emotions." I also believe there is an element of unawareness that plays into emotional eating. While at work, where people could see me, I would eat healthy fare – salads, spinach, Greek yogurt, seeds and nuts, vegetables – but when I would get in the car to go home, all bets were off.

I would call Andrew as I left the office so we could figure out dinner. "What would you like to eat tonight?" I would ask.

"I don't know. What's on your way home?" he would reply.

"Well, there's Chick-fil-a, Panera, California Tortilla. Any of those sound good?"

Andrew would pick one or suggest something else, and as long as I thought it was healthy, I would order dinner and pick it up on my way home. I wasn't making mindful choices or putting real effort into giving my body the quality fuel it needed.

When I realized how unhealthy my habits had really become, I was shocked. I stressed mindfulness and good eating habits with my clients but was blind to my own habits.

I talked with my care team to try to figure this out. Each of them had been through something similar, and although none of them said "here's what you need to do," they each talked to me about their journey and what they did. Even though it was different, there were enough similarities that it helped me see I was not alone.

Eating My Feelings

Don't you realize that your body is the temple of the Holy Spirit,
who lives in you and was given to you by God?
You do not belong to yourself, for God bought you with a high price.
So you must honor God with your body.
1 Corinthians 6:19-20

I started the work I needed to do to figure out what triggered my emotional eating. My professional work had shown me, again and again, that when something wasn't right, you have to look for the root cause if you want to effect real change. Now I needed to do that for myself. What exact trigger made me turn to eat things that weren't good for me? When was I doing this?

Again, I went back to what I knew and tracked my trends, not just what I was eating, but also when, how I felt, who I was with, and so on. It didn't take me long to see that I ate when I was stressed, tired, and not feeling in control. I ate healthily in the morning and while at work, but when I got home, it was a totally different story. I walked in the door and felt that I needed to wind down, so I snacked. I would talk with Bryan and get agitated, and I ate whatever was handy. I would do work for the spa and my volunteer activities, and I ate. I crafted, and I ate. When I felt sad, lonely, happy, I ate. My eating was indiscriminate—I chowed down from bags and boxes, none of it healthy to give my body the fuel it needed.

Those few weeks of tracking and analyzing were truly eye-opening. It was shocking to see how incongruent I was. How was I going to turn this around? How was I going to live the walk and not just talk it?

∼

Once I was more aware of my emotional eating and when I did it, my next task was to understand why I did this to myself when I knew it wasn't healthy for me? What inspired such self-destructive behavior?

Part of me wanted to back away from these questions and go back to pretending my diet was fine. But I had started this journey to figure things out for my life, so I couldn't let myself stop now. I didn't want to go any farther out of my comfort zone, but on some level I knew I had to push forward and really look for the deep answers to the questions surrounding my emotional eating habits.

After more talks with my care team, I went back to the idea of asking myself questions. With help, I came up with five concrete ones to work on:

1. Who are you?
2. What have you accomplished?
3. What do you like about yourself?
4. What don't you like about yourself?
5. Where the hell do you want to go from here?

As I wrote the questions on paper, my brain told me, "Oh, this won't take long, you've done this exercise before. It will be a piece of cake." Here were my initial answers:

Who am I? I'm a middle-aged widowed mother of three who owns a business, is very involved in the business community, promotes her professional industry with passion, provides leadership for her church, is a friend to many, has an award-winning marketing background, and makes handmade crafts.

What have I accomplished? I raised three children. I run a business. I was elected to the boards of two professional organizations. I am a board-certified colon hydrotherapist, a certified lay minister, a certified marketing director, a wellness advocate, and a detox specialist. I was named best day spa and best holistic practitioner in Bucks County, Pennsylvania. I was named colon hydrotherapist of the year, two-time FBLA national businessperson of the year, and won two outstanding marketing program awards. I developed award-winning marketing campaigns that achieved millions in sales, rolled out national product lines, and implemented shopping center grand re-openings in five states.

What do you like about yourself? I like to learn. I am a good friend and a good listener. I am an educator and a good presenter. I am fashionable. I get things done.

What don't you like about yourself? What's not to like? I am an overachiever!

Where do you want to go from here? I would like to work for ten more years, make lots of money, and then retire so I can travel and be with my kids. Beyond that, I want to be happy.

No sooner did I complete my answers than the little voice inside, the one that had nudged me the first time I asked myself questions, nudged me again. *Go deeper*, it said.

Go deeper? I just spent the better part of forty-five minutes writing down my answers. I *couldn't* go any deeper. But just like the voice pushed me to look at my food intake, I had a moment of clarity where I realized that I needed to really wrestle with these questions; and wrestle I did.

I sat with those answers for a while. Then I started talking to others, asking them how they would answer each question about me. As you can imagine, I got a myriad of answers, but the one thing they all had in common was I needed to listen and start really thinking about my answers.

The whole process of looking deep within and answering tough questions honestly challenged me. Sometimes I opened a door in my mind to look for an answer and had to slam it closed because it hurt too much.

The most difficult door turned out also to be the most cathartic. It was the one that helped me to figure out who I was and who I wanted to be, and it was one I opened and shut many times before I finally stepped through the opening.

$$\sim$$

One night, almost two months into my search for answers, I struggled to figure out who I was. A mom. Yes. A daughter. Yes. A friend. Yes. A business owner; a volunteer; a woman of faith; a professional...yes, yes, yes, and yes.

A widow. Yes. And that hit me square in the chest.

A widow. Why did my husband have to die that day? Why was I left to raise our three kids alone? Why did I have to shoulder the challenges with our oldest son? Why had I never let anyone help me? Why did I stress over things because I was alone? Why had I said goodbye, but never really let myself feel the pain of that loss: the grief of what could have been but never would?

The door didn't open with a small crack this time. I yanked it off the hinges. My youngest son was out, thank goodness; I might never have gotten through this if he'd been in the house. I sat in the living room, alone, crying. And as I wept, I realized I had never truly grieved my husband's death. The tears and the heartache were almost unbearable. I relived that dreadful day in 2006 to the point that I did not want to go on anymore just going through the motions and silently bemoaning that I was alone.

Please don't get me wrong. I grieved when my husband died, but only for a time. I told myself I had to keep going, that I would find a new normal if I just stayed the course. And that was exactly what I did for the better part of ten and a half years until I finally unlocked the door of grief and met it head-on.

I cried for a long time; two hours or more. Finally, I thought I'd drained myself of all my grief. Then I took down a framed portrait of my husband that we kept in the living room, and I just stared at it. I remember asking how he could leave me like that, and how could he let me become so sad. I didn't get any answers, of course, but I did begin to feel a fragile sense of peace.

I began to talk out what I was feeling—yes to the photo! As I did, I could hear Dave's voice in the memories of happy times during our almost twenty-two years together...his laughter, his sense of humor, his questions. I had been deeply loved. It was time to let go of the anger and resentment I had unconsciously buried.

Wow. I'd thought I had dealt with my pain all those years before. I had never expected to find that I hadn't, but that realization helped me begin to really figure out who I was.

I don't believe that one moment or another in our lives defines us forever, but I do believe we have defining moments that shape who we can and do become. I believe that night was exactly what needed to happen in my life to begin the next phase of my journey forward.

That night began my journey of processing my grief. I still didn't understand why Dave had to die when he did, but I became more peaceful with my non-understanding. I knew that if he could have lived, he would have fought hard to see our children grow up and see us grow old together as we had planned. I knew that life would have had challenges if he had lived, and I knew that there were no promises that tomorrow was guaranteed. I also knew that he would have wanted me to go on living, not just surviving, because he was my biggest cheerleader.

~

As I moved through the process of getting at and through my grief, I questioned and cried. I got angry; I cried. I yelled; I cried. I laughed at some memories, I cried at others. I felt alone and lost; I cried. I saw happy times and sad. I saw milestones he missed, and I cried. I just let the tears fall, some silently and some violently. I grieved, really grieved, without caring if anyone saw me or how vulnerable it made me. I cried because I needed to release everything that had built up inside, everything I had not allowed myself to face and feel for so long.

I have always understood that grief is different for each person. What I didn't understand was what that truly means. Grief, defined as deep sorrow, takes on a life of its own depending on the person and the circumstances one is in. My grief was unexpected, unimaginable, and unfathomable, so I suppressed it because I thought it's what I had to do to take care of my kids. The more I stuffed my grief inside me, the more I slipped into the black hole that had become my life.

Until I looked honestly at my grief, my grieving process had simmered under the surface like a volcano waiting to erupt. It would bubble and make me uncomfortable, but then I would push it down, and it would sit at bay for a while until it bubbled up again, and I pushed it down again. Each time I stopped myself from truly grieving, I hurt myself on the inside—my well-being—a little more. Had I not made the decision to figure out what was happening to me, who knows where I would be today.

As I've said, I never really blamed anyone for Dave's death. After all, it was an accident. I did wonder, though, why the driver of the truck who caused the accident wasn't charged in the aftermath. I remember asking my friend and attorney that very question.

"Since Dave was not at fault in the accident, and the truck driver admitted he wasn't paying attention when he turned left in front of the oncoming car, why isn't he being charged?"

"Well, it's like this, Cathy," my friend said. "The truck driver didn't get up that morning and say, 'I think I'll get in my truck and turn in front of Dave Windland's car and kill him today.'"

"I get that," I said, "but isn't it still manslaughter when there's an accident, and someone dies?"

"It was an accident, plain and simple. He was given a traffic citation and had to appear before the judge, and he was found guilty of reckless driving. That puts points on his license."

"So he just gets to go about his life, after he took the life of my husband and my children's father?" I kept asking questions because I needed to know, even though at the time, I had no idea that it would be part of the process of self-healing at some point down the road.

"He may not be going to jail," my friend said, "but he has lost his ability to drive a truck, which is his livelihood. He also has to live with the fact that his reckless actions took another person's life. His actions have left a widow and three fatherless children in his wake." My friend paused, and then said, "That's pretty heavy, probably more punishment than charging him with a crime and putting him in jail."

I understood that on many levels, but as I began to truly grieve, that conversation gave me pause. Did I hate the man who had driven the truck the day Dave died? Did I blame him for his reckless driving? I had always said that I had forgiven this man, but did I really?

Grieving is different for everyone. I had grieved those first three weeks after Dave's death as I cried through the numbness. Then reality—scary as it was—took over, and I had to get back to work to keep a roof over mine and my children's heads and food on the table. I had to figure out how to be both mother and father to my kids. I had to stay strong so that I didn't appear to be vulnerable to the outside world. I pushed my emotions down a little farther each day until I thought I had dealt with the grief and could go on.

It's funny how the mind works. We can push our emotions aside and tell ourselves we're okay because we think we have to do it that way. The more we tell ourselves we're okay, the more the mind fills with "stuff" that keeps us from dealing with the real emotions, the reality of what it all means to our well-being and self-care. Over the years as I pushed my emotions aside, my self-talk became more negative, even though I thought I was positive. I thought things were going well, but in reality, I was slipping into a black hole, farther and farther away from the person I thought I was.

As I went through my process to understand what I had done over the years and what I needed to do to change my downward spiral, it took me weeks to get to a feeling of peace within and let go of my forced resilience, so the hole in my heart could really begin to heal. I had to unpack events and memories, and as I did that, I had to open doors to places I had long since closed off.

I've been asked, "What was your process? How did you learn to grieve so many years after the tragedy?"

I wish I could say, "Here's the formula to help you grieve." It would really make the process so much easier. But, life being what it is, the grieving process is not a "one size fits all" thing. Grieving is different for each person. Why? Because each person's grief is unique, even though there may be similarities in the way people experience it. There is no one way to deal with grief, so don't ever let someone tell you that there is. There is no guidebook, no rules, no protocol; there is only common ground.

For me, on the night I talked to Dave's photo, I arrived at a crossroads. I could either continue as I had for more than ten years, trying to pretend to be all right when I was anything but, or I could finally deal with my emotions and see where my life would take me. I decided that I wanted to be joyful; I wanted to live again.

As I went through the grieving process, I began to realize that my emotional eating was tied to unprocessed grief, and that, in many respects, I defined who I was based on my husband's death.

Sugar-Free

*So whether you eat or drink or whatever you do,
do it all for the glory of God.*
1 Corinthians 10: 31

On April 1, 2017 (no, it wasn't an April Fool's joke), I said no more refined sugar! It wasn't easy, especially since I had a teenage boy in the house, but my youngest son was actually a big supporter of what I was doing. He started reading labels and deciphering what supplemental fact bars were actually saying. Although he still wanted the chips and cookies for himself, he respected what I was doing and stopped asking me to buy them. He also stopped asking me to go get fro-yo regularly, a habit we had developed together over the previous year.

As the sugar detox began, I was still dealing with my grief and response to working through it. Work was busy, and slowly I realized I was not hiding in what I did, but was becoming energized by it again. I will never forget the day my marketing director (she was so much more than that, for sure!) and I were meeting, and she asked me if I really wanted to be at the spa. I listened to what she had to say and her observations and told her that yes, I absolutely wanted to be in my job. I thanked her for the honest feedback, telling her about my journey and what I had been learning. I told her about the changes I was experiencing and how thankful I was for it all.

Afterward, as I pondered that conversation, I understood the lengths to which I had gone to put on a façade for the world. Her question had initially taken me by surprise; in all honesty, I wasn't sure why she was asking it. But as I thought about our conversation more, I realized I had been missing in action from my own business. Ouch! I had been showing up each day and doing what I needed to do, but I hadn't really been present or engaged the way I could have been. As I contemplated her question, I realized that I needed—no, I *wanted*—to be about relationships and helping others, my staff included. I needed to take off the façade I'd put on, as quickly as I could, and engage myself in my work in a much bigger way if I was going to be the person I wanted to be.

During the remainder of that spring, I continued to talk with my care team multiple times per day and analyze what was happening in my life: feelings, actions, eating habits, interactions with others, and my activities. I also kept going back to the five questions I'd given myself that I had yet to answer truthfully. I still hadn't come up with answers that resonated with me.

A month later, I was still working on myself, but I had been without sugar for thirty days. By that point, I noticed I had more energy, which was great, but the most exciting thing for me was that I didn't wake up in the mornings feeling tired and sore in my joints. I could actually get up and get moving without feeling pain. I talked with my clients about inflammation in the body and how processed, refined sugar contributes to that, but I had never understood it for myself. I was amazed at the difference I felt in my body. More importantly, I did not want to turn back. I had made a conscious choice to cut refined sugars out of my diet, and now I was making a conscious choice to keep them out so I could continue to feel good.

Then I read an article that explained processed sugars in the body so that everything I was experiencing made perfect sense to me. The article said that refined sugar is more addictive than cocaine, and because the body can't effectively process the sugar for elimination, it can actually stay in the body, building toxicity. This can create inflammation in the joints and in the digestive tract, even on the cellular level. Moreover, the body can take over fourteen days—*two full weeks*—to begin to process any refined sugar you eat. This information gave me a lot to chew on (no pun intended).

In 2013, I'd attended a convention and heard a talk by dietary expert Brenda Watson. I revisited what I'd learned from her, and re-read her subsequent book *The Skinny Gut Diet Book*. Brenda spoke about the relationship between sugars and heart disease, and how the relationship one develops with food is critical to the quality of life and longevity. In fact, it's as important as the mind-body-spirit connection.

In *The Skinny Gut Diet Book,* Brenda wrote about the teaspoon tracker, and how this tool could help me make the changes I wanted and deserved. The teaspoon tracker helped me understand how much sugar was in the foods I ate. When someone wanted to lose weight, they should have no more than six-to-eight teaspoons of sugar per day. When someone wanted to maintain weight, they should have no more than eight-to-ten teaspoons of sugar per day. The teaspoon tracker allowed me to calculate the total number of teaspoons of sugar I ingested. What a simple, yet brilliant, way to be in touch with foods and take control of what I was actually eating.

To calculate the number of teaspoons of sugar in anything you eat, you need to know the total carbohydrates and the total fiber in the food, because carbs turn to sugars in the body and fiber burns up sugar. With me so far? Good. Once you have these amounts, you can calculate your daily sugar intake and know exactly where you stand when you choose to eat a particular food. Take the total carbs minus the total fibers and divide the difference by five; this is total teaspoons of sugar in that particular food.

Revisiting this information and implementing the teaspoon

tracker helped me tremendously. I also revisited sessions from a convention I'd attended in 2015 when I heard speakers from The Truth About Cancer talk about similar things. The message was pretty clear that refined sugars do nothing good for your health and simply by eliminating them from your diet you can change the way your body handles cancer cells and disease.[1]

I do believe that all disease begins in the gut. This theory was first put forward by Hippocrates (460-375 BC), who is regarded as the father of modern medicine. When we put processed, chemical-laden foods without nutritional value into our bodies, how can we stave off disease?

I'd known these things before, but was finally starting to see that I hadn't been living the things I taught my clients. When you sense that kind of disconnect between the image you present and what you actually know about yourself, this can make you feel like a fraud. As I continued to feel the benefits of a no-sugar lifestyle, I felt more confident and real about what I shared with my clients. It's uncomfortable to feel that you're putting a false front on, and I was grateful to experience more authenticity in my life and work as I aligned my own choices with what I advocated.

Hippocrates said that we should let "food be our medicine and medicine be our food." That statement, coupled with all that I was learning about myself, brought me to a new level of understanding and the need for self-care.

Food has always been an important part of my life: not just straightforward consumption, but savoring, enjoying the aesthetics, enjoying the preparation when I had the time to do so. But up until this point, I'd never internalized all the information I had about diet and how it affects the body, and I'd never understood exactly how consciously I needed to think about my dietary choices. It was no longer just about having a "balanced meal" and including all the food

---

1   https://thetruthaboutcancer.com/sugar-white-death/

groups, which is the rule I learned growing up. It was more specifically about choosing the right foods, the foods that nourished me,
and made me feel great. I talked with my clients about the foods
they ate and what that meant to their digestive health, but this was
the first time I really delved into what those ideas meant for me and
my well-being. This marked a big step for me in feeling authentic,
living my truth as well as "talking the game."

Focus on Health

I will never forget your commandments,
for you have used them to restore my joy and health.
Psalms 119:93

I still avoided opening the doors to my best life, even as I became more and more aware that doing so was exactly what I needed—and wanted—to find myself again. As I planned for a convention that spring, making buttons and giveaways and fun items for the silent auction we were holding, I also planned my last high school graduation party. That final graduation was the catalyst that had indirectly started this chapter of my wellness journey. Although I felt a little sad that my baby was graduating high school (and that meant growing up and really not needing me as much), I was truly thrilled for him.

Graduation day came. We held his party in the afternoon, hours before the actual ceremony, because I had to fly out first thing the following morning. I will say that food-wise, I did great, although I did have the tiniest sliver of a cake made especially for the occasion. I felt happy for my son, very proud of him for his honors, and proud of myself for only having a moment's sadness as he accepted his diploma. It was a wonderful day for him, and we were surrounded by family members and friends.

During the ceremony itself, as I sat in the big arena with the other parents and attendees, listening to the class speeches, I couldn't help but ache at the fact that Dave missed yet another milestone in the lives of our children. He would have loved that Andrew had graduated with honors, and he'd have been so proud of everything our son accomplished during his high school experience. I had a hard time keeping the tears from falling, and an even harder time deciding whether they were happy tears or sad ones.

Early the next morning, I boarded a plane bound for Las Vegas. It landed about two hours before I had to present a workshop at the I-ACT convention. I'd planned to use the flight to review my presentation one last time but wound up instead reflecting on the previous days with my son. As the cab pulled up to the hotel, I frantically reviewed my notes one last time.

Inside the hotel, I was greeted warmly by colleagues and congratulated on my son's graduation. Somehow, that helped me with my sadness. By the time I got into my session room and was introduced, I felt excited and passionate about being there.

My workshop was about networking to build your business, and it's actually one of my favorite topics because it's all about building mutually beneficial relationships, not just increasing the number of contacts you have in your Rolodex. (I've recently been reminded that no one uses Rolodexes anymore, but I'm not sure what to call them, so I hope you understand!) Many people told me they loved my presentation and learned a lot from it. I felt very energized afterward and appreciated the opportunity to share my knowledge and experience.

The rest of the weekend gave me even more impetus to continue my journey. Although I knew many people already and met lots of new colleagues, I still felt as though I could have been more present and more fully the person I was meant to be. Again, this dissatisfied, uneasy feeling baffled me. *What the heck is this about,* I asked myself, *and what am I supposed to do with it?*

Four out of five members of my care team were also at the convention. That weekend, I had the chance to talk with them about a lot of the emotional stuff I had been going through. One night, Beverley, Gail Marie, Tiffany, and I stayed up late talking, and I shared that I felt I needed to do something about my sugar cravings. Even though I was staying away from processed sugars, I still craved them, which was frustrating. As we talked about healthy lifestyle eating and finding the diet that worked for me, Beverley mentioned water fasting. I didn't know anything about it and wanted to know more.

Beverley told me about the book, *The Obesity Code,* and what she had learned by reading it. She explained that because of the processed world we live in, our bodies can become so overburdened that resetting insulin resistance is important to cleansing and releasing built-up sugars. (Note: this is not something you should try at home without fully understanding the process. You should also discuss it with your healthcare provider and get their guidance.)

With the help from my care provider, I embarked on a water fast at the end of June 2017. I had done liquid and juice cleansing before, so I figured I could do this, too. Day one went okay. On day two, I felt tired and headachy as I had expected; this was part of the detox process I experienced with other cleanses. By day five, I felt better but was totally exhausted, not just tired, actually exhausted, and I was thankful for the long holiday weekend. I began introducing green juices and bone broth into my diet on day six but still felt exhausted. I worried that I'd done something wrong. My care provider didn't think I had; that was good news. I would have hated to think I'd made a mistake in the process that was supposed to help me, and instead made myself feel worse!

The remainder of that weekend, I did realize I didn't crave sugar anymore! My energy level remained low, but I didn't mind that, given the relief of not craving sugars. My son went away for a few days, so I decided another go at a water fast might be helpful, but after three days I stopped, noting exhaustion again.

By this point, I had become pretty good at being a health

detective, so the way I was feeling got me thinking. If I had done the water fast correctly and the exhaustion levels didn't lift once I'd stopped, what was causing me to feel so drained? I researched why this might be happening, and about three weeks later, I mentioned it all to the chiropractor I was working with at the time. I told him I thought I might have adrenal fatigue. He listened carefully, asked a few questions, and said he thought I was on to something and should have tests done. Saliva and muscle tests were both effective for identifying adrenal fatigue.

Sure enough, I had adrenal fatigue. I had felt tired for years but kept eating sugar, which gave my body a burst of energy so that's how I kept going. Sugars masked my adrenal fatigue and kept my body from functioning properly, affecting things like sleep, focus, regulation of hormone production, true energy to get through the day, creative and cognitive thinking...you get the picture.

So many people walk through life with adrenal fatigue and never know it. I'll admit, I didn't truly understand it until I had a reason to. As difficult as the water fasting was, it brought my adrenal fatigue to the surface and got me asking questions I had never asked before. I looked at myself in whole new ways, which was exciting and energizing. And because I was actively figuring out what was happening in my body, in conjunction with my healthcare providers, I learned how to provide my body with what it needed and be my own best doctor.

I started taking a natural supplement specifically for adrenal support and changed my diet a little more to help "feed" the adrenals. The adrenal glands produce needed hormones and regulate the body's energy levels, so feeding them the right foods helps them function better, which helps the body's overall well-being. The dietary changes were simple as I was already eating fresh, leafy greens, and lean proteins. I simply increased these, increased my healthy fat intake, and began to be intentional about my daily vitamin C and B12 intake.

~

As I figured out yet another new normal to recover from adrenal fatigue, the eleventh anniversary of my husband's death came into full view. Over the years, the kids always wanted to be together on August 10. Although Bryan wasn't available that year, Jennifer and Dustin came home from North Carolina so we could remember and honor their dad and my husband. That particular year, we decided to go to the Philadelphia Zoo, a place Dave had always enjoyed taking the kids when they were little. Sometimes, he was a big kid himself!

It had been at least ten years since we had been to the zoo, so it felt like a new experience. So many of the exhibits had been renovated or moved, and we had fun exploring. We visited all the favorites—the monkeys, the polar bears, the lions and tigers, the giraffes, and the primates— and at each exhibit,t we shared fond memories of the last time we had been there with Dave. The kids were sad that we no longer had their animal keys, something they used to love to use to listen to recordings about the animals and exhibits throughout the zoo.

We went on a quest to find the children's exhibits that the kids had loved to visit with their dad. As we made our way to the back of the zoo, we learned the petting zoo had been moved. In its place, we found a beer garden. We all laughed because Dave would have loved that: beer in the zoo. What did we do? The only thing we could; we had a drink in his memory.

Sitting in the beer garden felt bittersweet. It was a time to remember, a time to honor, a time to let go, a time to move forward. That day felt like a day for new beginnings. It's hard to explain, but I didn't feel nearly as sad that particular day as I had been on the anniversary day previously. I looked at two of my kids, and while I acknowledged that they missed their dad every day, I also saw them living life with love and grace. They were as well-adjusted as possible, given the cards life had dealt them.

I am proud of the fact that, for the most part, my kids do not let their lives be defined by the loss of their father, and I am so proud of the loving, kind, caring people they are becoming. I knew their dad would be too.

As for me, that day was another step on my self-care journey. I continued to deal with my grief, positively accepting another stage, and not hiding from it anymore. Sitting in the shade at the zoo, laughing with the kids, I realized for the first time in a long time, I was at peace, truly at peace with where my life was. The next day, though, would bring another challenge: taking my youngest son to college.

~

Andrew was a planner, so he got things together pretty well for college move-in day and kept to a good timetable. He packed most of his school things in the cars when we got home from the zoo. The next morning, we only needed to add a few odds and ends.

We got on the road in good time for the three-hour trip from Levittown to Williamsport and arrived at the Penn College of Technology a little earlier than we'd planned. Jennifer drove with me, and Andrew followed us in his own car with Dustin. I was very impressed with the move-in process once we got to campus. Five student volunteers met us and quickly emptied our two carloads of stuff into large wheeled carts. They rolled the carts into the dorm elevators and up to the third-floor room where Andrew would live during his freshman year. Given my previous experience with college move-in days, this process was an amazing godsend.

Once upstairs in the room, we unpacked all of Andrew's stuff and organized his side of the room to figure out what else he needed or had forgotten. We then did a little shopping for necessaries and took Andrew back to campus for a mandatory dorm meeting.

The next morning, after breakfast, we went food shopping and stopped at the bookstore. Finally, it was time for some photos before we said our goodbyes.

"Do we have to do pictures?" Andrew asked.

"Yes," Jennifer replied before I could speak. "We need them to prove we were here with you, and that you really are a college student."

The photos we took that day are precious to me. They capture that summer, which seemed to have flown past, but at the same time was full of milestones and new beginnings. When we finished taking the pictures, I hugged Andrew.

"I love you," I said in his ear.

"I love you, too," he replied.

I stood back to look up at him. "You're going to do great," I said. "Daddy would be so proud of you and all that you've accomplished. Keep doing your best, and you'll always be a success."

He hugged me again. "Thanks for everything, Mom."

Finally, it was time for Jennifer, Dustin and me to go. "Call me," I told Andrew, as we headed out, "and let me know how your classes are going."

He smiled and waved goodbye. "I will, Mom."

I knew he wouldn't call, even though he said he would. Boys. The thought made me smile as I drove out of the parking lot and headed for the highway towards home. As I had just two days before, I felt very much at peace with all of this, even though I would miss my son terribly.

"He's going to be just fine, Mom," Jennifer told me.

"I know, sweetheart," I said. "I know."

Over ten months, something had changed. The idea of being an empty-nester, with no kids left at home, didn't scare me anymore. How had I become so peaceful? No, *when* had I become so peaceful? Change had occurred without my really noticing. It all started with a conscious choice.

What Do I Really Want?

Great are your purposes and mighty are your deeds.
Your eyes are open to the ways of all mankind;
you reward each person according to their conduct
and as their deeds deserve.
Jeremiah 32:19

I went back to the five questions I'd asked myself earlier, those core questions I'd had trouble answering honestly and had been letting myself avoid. Now all of the kids were out of the house and busy with their own lives, and it was just me and the two cats, Piper and Phoebe. What was stopping me? I cleaned up all of my crafting stuff, got the house into better order, and sat down to concentrate on figuring out myself.

I went through the questions again, one at a time. This time, I was determined to answer them as fully and honestly as I could. After I looked at each one, I thought about it deeply before formulating a real answer.

Who am I? Earlier, I'd listed myself simply as a middle-aged widow and a business owner. Now I looked at those answers again.

I was still middle-aged, but that didn't define me, because I felt younger at that point than I did seven years earlier when I'd bought the spa. I was still a widow, but that didn't define me because I was living, and I'd decided to live my best life and live it to the fullest. I was still a business owner, involved in the local business community and my profession, but I didn't want those aspects of me to define me either. So, I challenged myself, how should I define myself; how should I say who I am?

What I came up with that time was very different.

I am a vital, confident woman who loves her children uncon-ditionally; is passionate about her profession and business; is a child of God and wants to serve others; loves life no matter what comes her way and wants to live; and wants to share her knowledge and experience for the love of wellness.

I still wasn't sure if that was me. Did that describe the person I had found behind the doors I had kept tightly closed all those years? I decided I deserved to find out.

What have you accomplished? Earlier, I had focused on my pro-fessional achievements: buying the spa, becoming a successful colon hydrotherapist, winning awards. I'd also focused on the fact that I'd raised my three children without the support of a partner. Looking at this list again didn't negate what I'd written—I had accomplished all those things and more —but again, did my list fully describe what I'd achieved in my life? I decided it probably didn't.

I sat with this question a bit longer before I was able to arrive at an answer that helped me see more clearly who I was. Up until that moment, I defined my accomplishments by what I had been awarded: certifications, accolades, and honors. I hadn't looked closely enough at all of the *intangible* things I'd accomplished.

My new list included other things:

✦ *I strive to do the right thing with love and gratitude.* (Okay, I'd let this one slide for a while, but I had found it again, and that was an accomplishment!)

116

✦ *I make time for others and value my relationships. They are not one-sided, and they have depth to hold me accountable.* (Again, this was something I'd lost and found again; an accomplishment in itself.)

✦ *I have really solid relationships with my kids.* (Yes, one of the three was still in process, but we were continuing to work on it: another accomplishment.)

✦ *I appreciate my staff and colleagues and tell them so whenever I can.* (You guessed it: that was another thing I had lost and found!)

✦ *I am grateful for everything—and I do mean everything!—I have in my life.* (I had always felt this way but had not been acknowledging it daily for a while. Going forward, I would focus on living life in a place of gratitude.)

✦ *I get up each morning and thank God for the gift of a new day, and that I have another chance to make a difference in this life.* (I had not even realized I had fallen out of this habit until I dug deeply into my questions.)

My list of accomplishments really made me see exactly how much I had missed during all the years I spent just going through the motions. Yes, I had accomplished many things, but I needed to hold the intangibles as valuable as tangible things as I continued my renaissance.

What do you like about yourself? As I thought about this question, not much had changed from my original responses. I had said that I liked to learn, was a good friend and a good listener, that I was an educator and a good presenter. I'd also noted that I had good fashion sense and got things done. I couldn't really add anything deeper to this list. That fact made me feel a little sad, so rather than dwelling on it, I moved to the next question.

What don't you like about yourself? My initial answer to this felt like a slap in the face. *What's not to like? I'm an overachiever!*

How flippant and sarcastic could I get?

Was that how I wanted to be? Absolutely not! Yet there it was on paper, staring at me. I didn't like that one bit, and I didn't much like the attitude of the woman who had written it.

I had to go much deeper. As I did, I found real, tangible things about myself that I realized I could change to become a better human being.

I didn't like the sarcasm or the façade I put up when I felt vulnerable. I didn't like keeping people at arm's length or keeping a defensive and guarded attitude. I didn't like being pulled into gossip, or binge-watching Netflix every night, or the fact that I had wasted so much time, so many years, going through the motions in my own life. I didn't like the fact that I felt alone in a crowded room or that I didn't remind myself to take time to "be still, and know that I am God" (Psalm 46:10) I'd had that quote stenciled on my kitchen wall for years as a reminder to myself, and I had still failed to see it and act on it.

As I looked at this question, I felt I wasn't kind enough, grateful enough, humble enough, or loving enough...but I realized I could be.

That struck a nerve! I could be. Yes, I could! I could work on myself. I could turn what I saw as negatives into positives.

The time I spent answering those last two questions was invaluable. Between them, they also answered the fifth and final question: **Where do you want to go from here?** Before, I'd mentioned professional goals and a desire to travel. With this version, I changed my focus.

I wasn't where I wanted to be, but I wasn't a lost cause either. I could work on the things I didn't like about myself, and make changes. After all, I was the only one who *could* make changes in myself. I *could* choose to be alive and positive and loving and kind, all the things I wanted to be.

Let me pause for a moment and say that this whole process was far from easy. Actually, it was painful, though not as painful as opening the doors to begin with. I had to really look inside myself to find the answers. My superficial answers hadn't been enough, and I now understood that those close to me, those who truly cared about me, saw right through my façade. Thank goodness they did and loved me anyway!

~

There is no one way to deal with your emotions. You simply have to engage with them, understanding that they're not right or wrong: they are your feelings, and you must not judge them. It was hard work for me to go through this process of unpacking what I had so neatly packed up for so many years. I could have stayed right where I was, not liking myself very much, and I probably could have kept treading water reasonably well for the rest of my life. But, in dealing with my emotions, my feelings or lack thereof, I saw that I was missing the best part of me. I was only living half a life; I only shared part of myself with others and all because I didn't want to deal with my emotions, my fears.

I'm not one to wear my emotions on my sleeve, and often I hold back sharing about myself because I don't want to be vulnerable with people. Yet, facing my emotions—meeting the person I had become—and focusing on how to get to the person I wanted to be was key to opening up the emotional block I had erected. Facing my emotions meant I had to be vulnerable with myself to be in an honest relationship with *me*, the one constant person in my life. Only then could I develop meaningful relationships with my children, family, friends, and anyone else I encountered on my journey.

My care team helped me look at myself and guided me to understand that I had to make choices. I could stay where I was, or I could figure out what I needed to do to change. I arrived at a critical juncture, so I made a choice to look at each of my feelings, each reaction, each encounter, and ask myself what was happening. Why did I feel that way? If I didn't like how I felt, how did I want to feel? Was there something I could do or say to make it better? If my feelings weren't in alignment with what I wanted, I had to look at that.

When it came to how I reacted in certain situations...let's just say that was certainly an exercise in self-control. It's not usually the best idea to react first and think later, yet I found I'd begun to do exactly that, often, in recent years. I had to do a lot of self-talk and self-coaching to train myself away from gut reaction and into a thoughtful response. Sometimes I still react first, but I'm getting better. I've learned that it helps to concentrate on my breathing, to give myself time to think in any stressful situation.

I've also learned that in considering the different situations I encounter, I can find similarities between them, and therefore find areas in which I need to improve. Beverley, Gail Marie, and Suzanne have helped me learn that when I find myself in recurring situations that I don't like, I can only change me. I can only deal with my own emotions and how to go forward: I can't change or control what other people do. If something kept recurring and I didn't like it, or it didn't serve my journey, I had the chance to look at how I might change myself. Reflection and consideration helped me a great deal in building and healing my relationship with Bryan, during and after his challenges. I also think they helped me with my relationships in general.

Answering the questions I'd given myself, answering them fully and honestly, took time and energy and courage. I didn't always want to face what I found behind the closed doors, so sometimes I had to battle with myself to accept my truths. Answering the questions felt like a tug of war initially, but the process became a warm welcome home, as I arrived at the point of understanding myself and knowing where I wanted my life to go next.

Changing Times

Every good and perfect gift from above, coming down from the Father
of heavenly lights, who does not change like shifting shadows.
James 1:17

It was September 14, 2017, and I was in Doylestown, Pennsylvania, with my good friend Chris. More or less out of the blue, I told her, "I have to tell you two decisions I've made. I need you to hold me accountable for them. First, I'm going to put my house on the market and downsize, and second, I'm going to start dating again."

I didn't know how she might react. Even though I knew these were the right choices for me, I was scared that she might think I shouldn't, for instance, part with the house my kids had grown up in.

For a second, she looked surprised, but then she smiled. "Thank God," she said. "It's about time!"

She was truly happy for me, fully in support of my decisions. I can chuckle at the scene now, but at that moment, I simply felt a huge relief. I was finally going to move forward. I didn't have to fear judgment for it, and I was going to live fully again. I felt so supported in my decisions that an increased sense of peace and joy came over me.

I flew to St. Louis the next evening to meet my parents and drive to the Ozarks for a family wedding. On Saturday, I told my parents about my decisions. My mother responded almost the same way

Chris had, even with almost identical words. I then told two of my cousins at the wedding, and once again, got a similar response and best wishes for much happiness. I did chuckle this time to see how happy and relieved everyone else seemed to be about my news, but I did have to wonder how pathetic I must have seemed for years, refusing to continue my romantic life and holding myself back in every way.

No worries, I told myself. I wasn't going to dwell on past choices. Instead, I would focus on the future and whatever it might hold.

The process of self-care has taught me that we can't necessarily judge our choices as "right" or "wrong," but we do have to take responsibility for them, and we do have to move forward based on what we choose. In my case, I had chosen to focus on my kids, and then on my business and learning new things. Those decisions had led me to where I was in the fall of 2017. How could I bemoan them? How could I say they were wrong when they ultimately brought me to the dawn of a new day and a renewed sense of living? Of course, I couldn't.

~

Just one week after setting my new intentions and sharing them with those closest to me, I woke up and decided that on that day, I would get serious about my physical well-being. Specifically, I would look at my body and appearance.

I could say I was shocked when I stepped on the scale that morning, but that would be an understatement. I have never been one to obsess about weight or weigh myself daily, but I certainly did not like what the scale said that day.

I had never made a point of doing regular exercise. A leisurely walk here, a hike with the kids there: those things always satisfied me. Actually following an exercise program was just not my thing, even though I had worked with a personal trainer for a few months four years earlier. I believed following a strict regime just wasn't for me, but that morning, something inside told me it was time to get started. I weighed and measured myself and started walking.

Later that day, I flew to Florida for a three-day board meeting. I could never have guessed how exciting that weekend was going to be.

You know the saying, "be careful what you wish for?" That weekend, I came to understand just how wildly generous the universe can be when you dare to put your thoughts and feelings out there. On the first evening, our group went to a dinner show called Medieval Times. I love English history, and a knight in shining armor is always a good thing in my book. After dinner and the show, several of the actors were in the great room outside the arena for photo opportunities. Beverley wanted a photo. After we got one, he started talking with us.

"From where do you ladies hail?" he asked. His carefully-crafted English accent and Medieval-era speech patterns made me smile.

Beverley told him she was from Connecticut.

I said, "I'm from Pennsylvania."

"And what brings you to our noble joust this evening?"

We told him about the board meeting and why we'd decided to come to the show that evening.

"When do you return home?" he asked. "And what plans have you for the rest of your stay?"

We explained we still had a full day of meetings the next day, and then we would have some free time before leaving for home the following day. To my surprise, he turned to me and asked, "May I have your number?"

Wow! Talk about an ego boost! I had no idea how old he was, but I was pretty sure I was old enough to be his mother. Still, I wasn't going to lose my head.

"I'm not sure about that," I replied. I didn't think he could really be serious about his request, so I was ready to smile and walk away, but something prompted me to do something else.

"How about you give me your number instead?" I couldn't believe those words had actually come out of my mouth.

"As you wish, my lady!" he answered at once.

I watched in disbelief as he took a Sharpie out of his sleeve and held out his hand for the paper crown I'd worn during the show. When I gave it to him, he wrote his name and number on the back.

"I do hope you ladies enjoyed the show," he said, handing the crown back to me, "and I look forward to hearing from you."

Beverley told him we'd had a great time. I simply held up the crown and smiled as we walked away to find the others in our group.

Beverley, Tiffany, and I rode in the same car to go back to the hotel for drinks. The two of them dared me to call my Medieval knight. I didn't have anything to lose, so I dialed the number.

If he was surprised that I called him, he didn't let on. I invited him to join us at the hotel bar for a drink. He said yes.

It wasn't a date, but it didn't feel far from it. That made me realize I hadn't been on a date in thirty-two years. (Hard to believe, when I'm only thirty-nine...!) I felt like a fish out of water, but at the same time, I felt like a schoolgirl again.

I hadn't flirted with anyone in years. My brain raced as I tried to remember how it was done. Was it still the same after all these years? Was I really ready for this?

It was such a whirlwind of feelings that I'm still not sure how well I handled it, but by the time the evening was over, I felt giddy. In fact, I felt like a new person, ready to experience life, whatever it brought.

I came home from that weekend feeling as if my whole world had opened up around me. I kept on with my walking regimen every day, and as I did, I began to see glimpses of the life I wanted to live. I especially noticed the couples around me, chatting, holding hands, sharing time together. I could have that again. I knew I could.

I was excited to go to work each day, and more surprisingly, I was eager to walk every morning. I even noticed there was a bounce in my step all day long. Two weeks after I started my walking routine,

I weighed in and measured again. I was amazed when I saw I was down seven pounds and five inches! My clothes had gotten uncomfortable, not just because they were a little big, but because they didn't fit the person I was beginning to see.

By the time I flew back to Florida a week later for a short trip with my kids, I was down eleven pounds and nine inches, and I was laughing and smiling more than I could remember in recent years. I even had to update my wardrobe a bit to suit my new body. Now, when I looked in the mirror, the person I wanted to become looked back at me.

Inked

Stop judging by mere appearances, but instead judge correctly.
John 7:24

On my second trip to Florida that week, when my kids and I went together, we celebrated my daughter and son-in-law's second anniversary. Along with that, I was celebrating living again.

We spent four days at various parks, and for the first time ever, I was the fun mom! The first day, we all went to Sea World. We laughed, we walked, we went to shows, and as we walked to see the stingrays, we passed a Henna tattoo station.

"I think I'm going to go look at that shop," I announced, as the kids started petting the stingrays.

Jennifer looked up with a raised brow. "Really? You're going to look at tattoos?"

"Yes." I smiled. "I'm just going to look at the designs," I said and walked off with a little bounce in my step.

I watched as an artist finished a design, and then I flipped through a book to see what other designs were available. I had never liked tattoos per se, but these designs, ornate and lovely with an Eastern flair, intrigued me. After a couple of minutes, I rejoined the kids and announced, "I'm going to get a tattoo."

Jennifer stared at me. "Who are you, and what have you done with my mother?"

I laughed.

She said, "Are you serious? I mean, I know it's just Henna, but I never thought I'd see you with a tattoo. What brought this on?"

"I just thought it would be fun," I told her. "They have this one design I think will look really pretty on my forearm. Come with me and see what you think."

She and I went back together. The tattoo artist reassured me—I think partly for my daughter's benefit—that the Henna was only temporary and would last up to two weeks.

"Okay," I said. "Let's do it."

Thirty minutes later, I had my first tattoo. The intricate band of delicate lines and dots did look lovely around my arm. Somehow doing this simple act made me feel young and daring.

The kids loved it and cheered for me. "All right, Mom!" We laughed and high-fived.

The next day, we split up and went to two different parks. Jennifer and I went to Epcot for the International Food and Wine Festival. It was a hot, sunny day. We sampled food and drinks and chatted with the people we met. While we waited in line for drinks in Germany, we talked with a man who was about to propose to his girlfriend. At his invitation, we took pictures of the proposal. We pulled pearls in Japan, took photos in Italy, and made friends with people from all over the globe. I couldn't recall such a day full of smiles and laughter.

Together, we went to the Animal Kingdom on the third day, and to Disney Springs that evening, where we enjoyed Irish music and dancing, good food and lots of laughter. I'd offered to let the kids go by themselves to Disney Springs without their mother tagging along, but they all told me they wanted me to come too. I could tell they genuinely wanted us all to spend time together; they didn't feel obligated to have me around, the way they sometimes had in the past.

We spent the last day at the Magic Kingdom. The place was

packed, but we still had a great time at the parade and on the rides. We stood in line to see the Disney Princesses and took pictures with each one, and took the obligatory pictures in front of the castle, too. Later, we watched musical presentations and looked for shirts along Main Street just to get out of the heat for a few minutes. All in all, we had a wonderful, carefree time together.

I knew I had finally become the fun mom: you know, the mom the kids want to hang with, not because they have to but because they like spending time with her. The kids were all old enough that they could have gone off on their own, but every time we did something together that weekend, we laughed heartily and with joy. It felt good to be that kind of mom.

My kids were fully supportive of the new me; they were happy about all the changes I was making in my life, and even encouraged me to date and have fun. My youngest reminded me that two years earlier, he had told me to get online because "on Match.com, two out of three every matches ends in marriage." I wasn't sure I was ready to get quite that serious, but it was great to know that my kids were cheering for me, every step on my new journey. That trip was a special time I'll always remember.

$\sim$

During that fall, part of my self-care practice included reading thought-provoking books. I don't quite remember how I found it, but it was amazingly eye-opening and helped me to look at myself in more new ways. It talked about posture, wardrobe, appearance, relationships, communication, and female sexuality. It gave me so many ideas that I read it three times in a row, cover to cover.

It's called *The Good Girls Guide to Bad Girl Sex*. Now, don't judge a book by its title! It's not a sex book. It's about finding your sexual self through your clothing, voice, looks, etc. It's about getting in touch with yourself, loving yourself, and letting that love shine through in everything you do, and figuring out the totally authentic you.

I've always felt that I had a good sense of style, but this book made me take a fresh look at my wardrobe. I had lost enough weight after five weeks that I needed new clothes that fit, but as I looked in my closet, I didn't see anything I wanted to continue wearing. As I began the arduous process of shopping, I began to try on styles that I would never have looked at in the past. To my surprise, I found that I looked good!

After a couple of shopping excursions, I decided that I needed to put on a new attitude toward clothing. I was going to buy nothing but items that made me feel sexy: not trampy or sleazy, but sexy as in, "I feel really good about myself." As I continued to lose weight and inches, I found a new, up-to-date, classy style that was all me. Every time I bought a new item, I would clean out at least two in my closet. It was a very cleansing experience, and as I did it, I realized I had become complacent and frumpy over the past several years. Without even realizing it, I'd stopped caring about my appearance. As I examined how I felt, I realized my new outlook was exactly where I needed to be, and the cleansing of my wardrobe was a good thing.

The book helped me to face not only my relationship with clothes but also my relationship with *me*. I had to be comfortable in my own skin and love myself. The wardrobe was like a window dressing: was I showing the self I wanted to show to the world?

It was really interesting to watch how people responded to me as I began to care about my appearance and update my style. I received compliments on my hair, even though I hadn't changed the style at all, and how my eyes looked brighter and had a sparkle. Although I didn't make huge changes, I did take a few more minutes as I got ready each day; I put a little more effort into putting myself together.

The Good Girls Guide also helped me reclaim my feminine confidence. In my younger years, I was always confident and had a positive outlook on just about everything; nothing held me back, and I was going to conquer the world to make a difference. As I read and reread this book, I wondered how I had gotten so far from that young woman filled with confidence and poise and chutzpa. In recent years, my confidence had developed a bitter edge to it, something I never saw but that definitely rubbed some people the wrong way. At this point in my life, I figured I had nothing to lose and decided to let my confidence exude in everything I did.

I took care selecting my clothing: nothing but what made me feel sexy. I took more care in applying my makeup lightly, but with purpose, and doing my hair. I walked into a room standing tall, and I spoke with a smile in my heart. I had a clarity of purpose for the first time in a long time, and I felt like a whole new person.

People responded really positively to me. Whether it was a business colleague or employee, client, or friend, I never got tired of hearing the positive feedback, and still appreciate it to this day. And for the first time, I took pictures of myself gladly. I'd never liked documenting myself, but now I wanted to remember this newly confident and happy woman.

Welcoming Love

There is no fear in love. But perfect love drives out fear,
because fear has to do with punishment.
The one who fears is not made perfect in love.
We love because He first loved us.
1 John 4:18-19

Before I'd left for Florida for the trip with my kids, I'd had a dream, the first dream I could remember in any detail in eleven years.

I knew I was dreaming because I remember thinking it was a really long dream, and I wanted to wake up. The remnants of the dream that stayed with me after I awoke, including having a conversation with my late husband. I told him, "I miss you, and I wish you were here."

He smiled and said, "It's time. Go forward."

I guess if you are going to have a dream, it's good to have one that helps you to gain some clarity, some hope for the future. When I finally did wake, I felt I was on the right track and that, yes, I was meant to live again.

When I told my care team about the dream, their responses were warm and positive.

"That's beautiful. You know that he's happy you're living again and transforming into the woman you're meant to be."

"He's confirming that you're right to live a new life."

"He's telling you it's okay to live again!"

I never realized until that moment that, while I did want to feel peaceful about my decisions for my family and myself, getting that confirmation affirmed that I would be okay. I took another step through my grief, and I was still alive.

The Good Girls Guide book also helped me realize that the most important thing I could do was to show up to life for *me*! I was enough: I could and needed to love myself for who I was and who I wanted to be. I didn't need anyone else to complete me. I wasn't supposed to live for my kids or anyone else: I had to live for myself, fully, or else I would only be going through the motions. *The Good Girls Guide* gave me another reason to know I was headed in the right direction with my new life.

~

Self-care always means making choices that let you live your best life. When I got back from the Florida trip with my kids, I took two more steps on my journey. First, I reached out to my former trainer, Shari-Beth. I explained to her what I was doing and that I needed to do more to support my physical health. I wanted to get back into the strength training that she and I had done together four years before, but I needed reminders of what we'd done. I also needed the accountability of working with someone. I asked Shari-Beth if we could do a boot camp that would get me back on track, and she agreed. It was great to add another person to my care team, someone who brought a different kind of accountability to my journey.

What a kick! My daily walking gave me time to myself to think about things, do audio devotionals, and push myself to go farther, faster, or both. I tracked my steps and time, walking outside until the days got shorter and the mornings were too dark and cold, and then I walked on my treadmill in the garage. Twice a week, I worked out with Shari-Beth, using whatever equipment I had at my house: an exercise ball, a mat, bands, and eight- and ten-pound weights. She and I met virtually, so I didn't have to go to a gym. She encouraged me to keep working toward my goals, celebrated my victories each week, and checked in to make sure I was eating the right foods and giving my body the nutrition it needed to sustain the weight and inch loss I experienced. Even though I'd never believed an exercise regimen could be right for me, my motto truly became "Bring it on!"

During this time, I continued to live a full and busy life: running a business, working as a practicing therapist, downsizing the house, and spending time with family and friends. Then came the second new step on my journey. I reached out to a friend of mine who is a professional matchmaker, and I told her I was ready to start dating again.

As we talked, she asked me a lot of questions about my goals and hopes for a new relationship. Some of her questions I could answer, and others I had only begun to think about. At the end of our conversation, she announced that I needed to get online and have some fun: get my dating sea legs, so to speak, in a strictly casual environment.

I was taken aback. *Online dating? Really?* But I listened to what she said. She explained that I needed to take things gradually, stay relaxed, and have fun with dating, as I had been while rediscovering myself. Online forums would allow me to do just that. I could chat with guys on the sites and then decide when I wanted to meet someone in person. I didn't feel totally sure this would be right for me, but I decided she was the professional and knew better than I did.

I got myself onto two online dating sites, and I have to tell you, I felt right away that it wasn't my scene. I was confident in myself and wanted to meet people, but I didn't like having to answer all the questions the sites asked for and fit myself into their categorized boxes.

Still, I did my best to respond to the questions so someone might be interested in getting to know me. Within a day of posting, I began getting notifications that people were checking out my profile and messaging me. Although I'd decided I would see this process through for a least a couple of months, some of the guys who sent me messages were, shall we say, not what I wanted in a companion at all!

I didn't let myself give up quite yet. My son Andrew was glad to hear I was trying out online dating, but he felt concerned about me giving out my phone number, so he suggested I get an app on my phone called Text Free. He explained that the app would give me a new phone number without my needing to get another phone, and no one would be able to trace me through this number. It sounded a little strange to me, but he told me it was for safety. I followed his advice and kept chatting with guys online. Finally, when I felt ready to talk with a few matches offline, I had my new phone number ready to give out. As it turned out, it was nice to use the new number because I could distinguish "dating" calls easily.

Several of the guys I connected with seemed nice, but I only met a couple of them in person. While I did have fun talking and flirting, I ended up feeling that online dating was not for me. I know plenty of people who met their spouses online, so I'm by no means against it. I just didn't feel entirely comfortable with having everything online, and knowing that some of the people I met might not be telling me the truth about who they really were meant this wasn't my scene.

Through that experience, I realized that I'm very much a people person. It works best for me to meet and connect with people face to face; I found it hard to get to know someone through online chatting or texting. Even though it didn't result in any lasting relationships, the nearly two months I spent online gave me another learning experience and another step in my journey. Also, as my friend, the matchmaker, said, it gave me the chance to ease back into the dating scene to see what I wanted.

Sometimes we need to take time to mark milestones in our lives and celebrate where we are, where we've come from, or what we've come through. I wasn't used to celebrating myself, as a rule, but my journey to self-care taught me that I needed to honor the smaller steps along the way, instead of waiting until everything was perfect or exactly the way I thought it should be. I had set a goal for myself to lose forty pounds total, so when I reached the milestone of twenty pounds and eighteen inches lost, I decided it was time to celebrate.

I've never been a big fan of tattoos and never understood the purpose. In fact, when Jennifer got her first tattoo at nineteen, I was hurt and did not talk to her for several days. I know it was childish of me, but I was in a bad place.

Since beginning the physical side of my self-care journey, though, I'd found myself interested in tattoos. When I was with clients or friends who had them, I asked questions about them: things like what is the meaning, why that design, why that placement, when did you get it, did it hurt, and so on. The Henna tattoo I got on my second Florida trip was really beautiful. Although it only lasted for a couple of weeks, it prompted so many conversations that I started thinking about getting a permanent tattoo to celebrate my journey back to me.

As a detoxification specialist, though, the idea of getting a real tattoo gave me a crisis of conscience. Putting ink into my body could mean adding toxicity when I had been working so hard to eliminate toxins. I researched my options. First, I learned that tattoos could be made with vegan ink. Then I found an artist in my area who used vegan ink exclusively. I got in touch and asked a lot of questions. Then went back to a few friends who had ink and asked them questions too. Finally, I did the only thing left to do: I called my daughter.

The conversation stayed casual at first. I told Jennifer about work, and packing up the house, and how my workouts were going. Finally, as nonchalantly as I could, I said, "In fact, I'm so excited about my progress I've decided to get a tattoo."

"What?" Her shock and excitement ran down the phone line to me. "No way! Really?"

I promised her it was true.

"Okay, Mom," she said. "If you're going to do it, you have to take me with you!"

I told her I'd made my appointment for November eleventh.

"Good," she said. "I'll plan my trip home for that weekend. I think I'll get another tattoo as well."

We talked about it some more, but it wasn't until she came home in November and we went to the appointment together that she finally told me why she'd really wanted to go with me. She didn't particularly want a new tattoo, or to sit there while I got mine, but she'd been afraid I wouldn't actually go through with it, and she was determined to make sure I did!

My tattoo design used a Celtic symbol for new beginnings and flowers for new life. I created a draft of it and sent it off to the designer, who did a fabulous job of getting it just the size I wanted. By the time she finished, I celebrated where I was and where I was going from that moment forward: there was no turning back, not that I wanted to. The milestone my new ink celebrated wasn't just the weight loss, because that can come and go. I marked a new beginning, my new life.

I now believe that we need to celebrate life every day, in every way possible. We aren't meant to live under a cloud, yet so many of us do, for whatever reason, sometimes without even realizing it. I was one of those people. I celebrated big things—holidays, the kids' birthdays, graduations—but when it came to small things, I just let them slip into oblivion. As I look back, I can see that I didn't celebrate the little things in life because I didn't think I deserved to. I also knew how to celebrate other people's accomplishments, but never my own.

I made intentional choices to change that. Redefining my sense of style, getting a tattoo, reclaiming my sense of femininity, smiling from within, moving for the sheer joy of moving, dancing like no one was watching, laughing simply because I could: all of these were ways for me to celebrate life, my journey, *me*.

~

Every day we have choices to make. Will I get out of bed? Will I go to work? Will I be happy? Will I make a difference today? Will I be grateful? Will I be positive? Will I be kind? The list could be seemingly endless and include all kinds of questions, but the single most important thing I've learned is that the way we answer those questions is *our own choice*. We choose, and we set our *intentions* for the day.

For example, we can do the following:

+ *I choose to get out of bed and live an awesome day!*

+ *I choose to get to work, make an honest living, and support myself.*

+ *I choose to be happy simply because I am me, and I do not depend on anyone else for my happiness.*

+ *I choose to make a difference in my community today.*

+ *I choose to be positive.*

+ *I choose to be kind and encourage those I come in contact with, to lift them up.*

+ *I choose to be grateful and live life in gratitude for all the blessings—big and small—that I have received.*

+ *I choose to live my life as my best self, incorporating what I believe and what I learn, so that I will always keep moving forward on my journey.*

I choose. I choose. I choose.

In choosing the way I live each day, I can set my destiny on the path I determine. When we consciously make choices about our lives, we can effect change. First, though, you have to make sure your "why" is strong enough.

When I began this journey, my "why" was the fear of being alone, really alone, for the first time in thirty-two years. I was afraid of having to spend time with someone I did not really like and afraid of dealing with the "stuff" I had pushed down for so many years. I didn't know if I could get through that. Yes, I chose to embark on a journey when I had no idea where it would lead, but I had to do it to save myself from falling into deeper darkness.

That was a huge choice to make. My tattoo, celebrating my weight loss milestone, was a smaller choice, but it felt liberating. I didn't do it for anyone but me! I did not care if anyone ever saw my ink or knew what it stood for: it only mattered that I did it for myself, and I knew what it symbolized. I smile each time I see that tattoo or think about its meaning, so in a small way, the celebration continues. Yes, life's small things are meant to be celebrated and celebrated often!

This brings me back to the idea of the mind/body/spirit connection as the foundation of wellness. When I first bought my business and heard that concept, I didn't really understand what it meant. Through study, seeking knowledge, and going through personal trial and error, I've come to understand that we need to have a balance to enjoy true wellness: balance of the mind (emotions), body (physical), and spirit (something bigger than self).

Every time I talk about the mind/body/spirit connection, I use the example of a three-legged chair. As long as each leg has the same amount of attention, the chair stays upright and balanced, but if you take away any one of the legs, the chair will fall because it cannot balance on just two legs. The mind/body/spirit connection is the same way. If we focus on only two of the three sides, we will not be in balance; our well-being will be off-kilter to some degree. That's an unhealthy way to live for any length of time.

I had gotten out of balance in my own life without realizing it. I'd focused on all three sides of my mind/body/spirit connection, but not all at the same time and not to any degree to truly effect change.

I always thought I did well on the spiritual side, but even that had moments of sluggishness if I am honest with myself. And let's face it, self-care has to be brutally honest to be all you need it to be!

As I reached the newest milestone in my journey, celebrating the smaller things in life, I felt I was focusing on my mind/body/spirit connection in new and deeper ways. I felt a sense of connection, of balance, that I had never felt before, at any point in my life. I was full of true joy and peace. I felt more comfortable in my own skin, more confident in who I was becoming, and more connected to others than ever before because I was connecting with myself all the way around. I made a choice to change because **my "why" was big enough**—scary enough—and along the way, **I became worth it**!

My house went on the market at about the same time that I got my tattoo. It felt strange to see a "For Sale" sign in the front yard every day, but I knew I'd made the right decision.

The holiday season came upon us just a week later, and I needed sweaters for colder weather. I was always up for a good shopping trip, and this one was very exciting: I was now down two sweater sizes, three pants sizes, and four dress sizes. I had fun trying on clothes and sharing part of my journey with the sales associate as we chatted. I was in such a good place that Thanksgiving, giving thanks and celebrating with pure gratitude in my heart.

Christmas that year was all about family togetherness, friends, and extended family, rather than buying gifts and trimmings. I still decorated and sent out cards, but I did it in a new way, a smaller yet classic way that I absolutely loved. You might say that streamlining the holidays actually increased the joy: less is more!

In fact, I cannot remember celebrating the holidays so minimally large in many, many years, maybe even since I was in school. We spent Christmas itself at the family farm in Central Illinois; that was our last Christmas at the farm because my parents moved to an apartment eight months later. It was such a joy to be surrounded by family and friends, some of whom I hadn't seen in years except on Facebook. We reconnected, chatted, and shared stories. I was also extremely grateful to share that holiday with my care team member Tiffany and her husband Jason, who joined us from California. Sharing Christmas snow and below-zero temperatures, as well as small-town life with them, was such a gift. That Christmas, just as I had been learning to do since my announcement to rejoin the human race just three months prior, I chose to be happy. Each day was filled with love, laughter, good cheer, and fun: each day was filled with blessings.

The holidays marked the end of that calendar year, 2017, but they put an exclamation mark on the new beginning I had started. I had come through so much, and here I was: happy, healthy, and enjoying life. My loved ones and I shared moments that we'll always have in our hearts. Our celebration was full of warmth and joy...even though it was eight degrees below zero!

Two days after Christmas, as I left my childhood home and began the drive back to Pennsylvania, I had a sense of calm that I had not felt in more than a dozen years. I had made this trip several times, but this time the trip east was filled with new excitement and opportunities. I reflected on the past year as I drove across I-70 to the Pennsylvania Turnpike. Just twelve months earlier, I had been scared and not sure why. I'd realized I didn't like the person I had become, but I didn't know how to change. I'd learned that I wasn't living my life congruently with my work and beliefs, but I didn't know how to repair that.

As I drove, I understood that my journey had begun with a single choice: the choice to say, "Why do I feel this way?" After that came the choice to listen and find out what was going on with me; to be the detective I needed to be to decide who I could become. As I reflected on all that I had come through, I realized that every single situation I had been through, every single fear I had faced, every single wall I had climbed was for my own good. They had let me appreciate

THE GIFT OF LOSS

the human struggle and condition and become a better version of myself. I realized I couldn't have side-stepped any of it: I had to come through it! And I think I am better for it, better for myself, and more importantly to my servant's heart, for those I come in contact with, whether it is for a moment or a lifetime.

That drive home gave me lots of time to think. As I reflected over the past year, I thought about the next few days and going into the new year. Yes, I had to return to work, which would be great. I also thought about the fact that I had a blind date that Friday night, which the matchmaker had set up right before I left for Illinois.

I only knew my date's first name and that he was a holistic chiropractor who lived an active lifestyle. I decided that no matter whether we really clicked on the date or not, we could always talk about our businesses and maybe become referral sources for each other.

On Friday, December 29, 2017, I finished work mid-afternoon and headed home to get ready for my date. What to wear? I think I changed outfits three times before settling on a conservative yet elegant one. As I prepared to leave for the restaurant, I texted my date to let him know I was on my way.

Remember that my son had set me up with the Text Free number for dating? I must have been nervous that night, because I didn't think about it and texted from that number, yet I'd given him my cell number. After all, the matchmaker had vetted him for me. Anyway, as I was driving to the restaurant, my phone rang.

"Hi, Cathy," the voice said when I answered. "This is Jerry."

A New Beginning

Rejoice always, pray continually, give thanks in all circumstances;
for this is God's will for you in Christ Jesus.
1 Thessalonians 5:16-18

"Hi, Jerry," I said. "Nice to hear your voice." To myself, I thought, *Nice voice, for sure.* It was warm and clear, friendly.

"Did you just text me?" he asked. "I got a message but didn't recognize the number, so I was calling just to confirm we were still on for dinner. I got to the Yardley Inn a few minutes ago."

I tried not to let him hear how flustered I felt. "Oh, yes, that was me. I'm sorry, I have two numbers, and I thought that was the one I'd given you." How embarrassing! Would he think I was a little goofy? Oh, this didn't bode well. I had to tell myself to stay cool. "I'm just a couple of minutes away," I said.

"Take your time. Our table is ready whenever you get here." I liked his relaxed attitude. "What kind of car are you driving?" he asked. "I'll meet you at the door."

I had to admit to myself, that was pretty charming. "I'm in a silver Town & Country." By then, we had actually talked long enough that I said, "I'm just about to pull into the parking lot in the valet line."

"I'll see you in a minute."

As I got out of the car and walked around to the restaurant entrance, I saw two guys standing there. Which one was I meeting?

Thankfully, one walked towards me around another group of people headed inside. "Cathy?"

I smiled. "That's me."

"Hi. I'm Jerry. Thanks for coming out on such a cold night."

As he came closer, I got a good look at him. Not too tall, but well-built; he looked like he worked out often. Distinguished-looking gray hair. Green eyes. And what I liked best: a ready, genuine smile.

"I'm glad to meet you," I said. "And actually, this is a heatwave compared to where I've been this last week. It was eight degrees below zero when I left Illinois on Wednesday morning."

He chuckled.

Was that good, I wondered? I was so out of my element dating in a new century.

"Let's get inside," he said. "Our table is ready."

I wish I could tell you that sparks flew between us in those first few moments, but they didn't, really. It was just a pleasant way to meet someone new: a real date! Once we got inside, he took my coat to the coat check and then told the hostess we were ready to be seated. The restaurant was busy and filled with lots of energy. The hostess escorted us to a table for two near a window, where we had a view of the river and the beautiful outside lights.

Our server came over and told us her name was Courtney. She looked to be around college age. She took our drink orders and disappeared again.

"So you went to Illinois for Christmas," Jerry said.

"Yes," I said. "My youngest son and I drove out to the family farm to be with my parents, and my daughter and son-in-law and friends from California flew in as well."

"I just got back from a couple of days skiing in the Poconos," he said. "My daughter was supposed to go with me, but she had to cancel at the last minute. So I went by myself."

I liked that he'd felt confident enough to enjoy an adventure by himself. "How was it, skiing alone?" I asked.

146

"Lonely, but good, and bitter cold. I love to ski, though," he said.

Courtney came back to the table with our drinks. I noticed how polite Jerry was, pausing our conversation to be sure he thanked her before she went on to the next table. We'd just started to talk again when she reappeared.

"Can I take your order?" she asked.

Jerry laughed. "I don't even know her last name yet, Courtney. How can I order?"

I liked his easy sense of humor, and the way he'd admitted he'd been too busy talking to me to look over the menu. Poor Courtney wasn't sure how to respond, so she said, "Oh, I'll come back in a few minutes...take your time," and then hurried away again. We laughed and decided we'd better look at the menus.

The historic Yardley Inn on the Delaware River is one of my favorite restaurants. I had a pretty good idea already of what I wanted to eat, but as we surveyed the options, I asked, "Do you like Brussels sprouts?"

"Yes," he said promptly. "I love them."

"Would you like to share some? They're really good here."

"That would be great."

Okay, I thought, *someone who likes Brussels sprouts.* That was a pretty rare breed in my experience. I had a feeling this was going to be a good evening.

Courtney returned a short while later. She came up to my side of the table this time, and said, "May I ask you a question?"

"Sure," I said.

"Is this really your first date?"

I smiled. Before I could answer, Jerry jumped in with, "Why would you think it wasn't? I don't lie."

I laughed. Courtney glanced back and forth between Jerry and me. "I'm sorry," she said. "You just both looked so comfortable with each other, I couldn't believe it was really the first date."

We assured her it was, and a blind date at that, and went ahead to order appetizers and our meals. Honestly, other than the Brussels sprouts, I can't remember what we ate that evening.

I do remember what we talked about. We were so comfortable and easy with each other that Courtney was right: it was as if we'd always been friends. We talked about our work, vocations and avocations both. We talked about our children— it was interesting that we each had a girl and two boys—and the challenges of single parenthood, and how we had each become single parents. I told Jerry about Dave's death, and he talked about his difficult split from his ex-wife.

I found myself talking about Bryan, which surprised me. I didn't usually talk about those challenges with anyone, especially not someone I'd just met, but that night, it felt right. We talked about our shared faith, too, and found that we had numerous mutual acquaintances, colleagues, and friends. We couldn't believe that we'd never run into each other before this date. We laughed, we ate, and we enjoyed each other's company.

And then the evening came to an end. *What now?* I thought. *Should I ask him about getting together again? Do I tell him to call me? Do I ask if he wants to go get coffee?* I had absolutely no idea how this was supposed to go, but I knew I wanted to see him again.

He got my coat and gave the ticket to the valet, very gentlemanly of him. As my car drove up, he walked me outside. "Thanks again for coming out," he said. "It was nice."

What does that mean? "Nice" was such a neutral word. Had he really had a good time? Did he want to see me again, or did he feel like one dinner was enough?

I did my best not to act like a confused schoolgirl. "Yes, it was nice to meet you." We could both use that word. "Thank you again for a wonderful dinner. I enjoyed it."

He looked at me, and for a split second, I thought he was going to kiss me. I was ready to respond, but at the last second, he turned his head and simply hugged me.

Hmmm. He walked me the five steps to my car and opened the door for me. I got in. Before putting my key in the ignition, I said, "Thank you again for a lovely evening."

"You're welcome, and thank you too. I'll call you."

Is that how it's supposed to go? I couldn't remember. Right then, I couldn't figure it out; all I could do was drive home.

Had that been an anti-climax, there at the end? By the time I arrived home, I decided it was the twenty-first century, and I had every right to text to say thank you again, so I did.

"Hi! Just wanted to say thank you for dinner. I had a really nice time and enjoyed getting to know you a little. Look forward to talking again soon. [blushing smile emoji]"

About an hour and a quarter later, I received a reply. "Hi Cathy, you're welcome! You beat me to it. I planned to text you as soon as I got in, but my neighbor intercepted me in the cul-de-sac, and I had to make an appearance at his party. I also had a VERY nice time tonight. You were easy to talk to and I love your outlook on life. BTW, I never told you that you looked great. I look forward to speaking to you soon! Sweet dreams [smile emoji, zzz emoji]"

~

The next morning, the matchmaker messaged me to ask how everything went. I told her I'd had a great time, and I told her about the texts Jerry and I exchanged after the date. Since I didn't know the protocol of being set up by a matchmaker, I asked if I could text him and invite him to a holiday gathering at my house that evening. She said of course, so just after eight in the morning, I did.

"Hi, there! I'm getting ready for a holiday get-together at my house tonight and wanted to invite you to stop by if you're able. Nothing fancy, just a bunch of friends and colleagues for casual fun. [smile emoji]"

I knew he was seeing patients that morning, so I didn't expect an immediate response. One came at 12:37 pm. "Really? I'd be happy to come. I'm finishing my notes. Can I call you after 1:15ish?"

"Absolutely!"

He called, and we chatted for a while. I gave him directions, which he wrote down because he's "old school," and he said he looked forward to seeing me that evening.

Can you imagine the scene for just a moment? Here I was, a grown woman with three nearly-grown children, and I was absolutely ecstatic that this man I had just met would be coming over that evening. I went through the rest of the day, smiling from ear to ear. I had always loved hosting my holiday gatherings, but that day I was filled with excited anticipation for something new and unexpected.

Jerry arrived at my house an hour after the party started. I greeted him at the door, and this time he kissed me hello.

He smiled and proceeded to tell me I gave him the wrong directions. What? I had been giving the same directions to my house for more than twenty-five years, how could I have given the wrong directions? He explained.

"I left the paper with the notes I'd written at home, so I was going from memory. First, you told me it was the third right when it was the fourth off the main road. Then, you told me it was the sixth house on the left on your street, but it's on the right. I went to the house across the street, and when I rang the bell, a young Asian man answered. I didn't remember you saying anything about that, but I thought 'okay' and said I was here to see Cathy. The young man turned and called for Abbey, which I thought was odd. A young girl came to the door, and I explained that I was here for Cathy's party. She looked at me a little funny and then said, 'you must mean Cathy across the street.' Awkward!"

I laughed and explained that my neighbor's name was also Kathy. Then I had to tease him a little about how his memory was definitely worse than my directions. We went inside, and I introduced him to some friends. It turned out that he already knew a couple of people there and found connections with many others. Everyone had a great time.

After everyone else left, we stayed in the living room talking and getting to know each other more. In the middle of our conversation, he quietly said, "You know, I prayed for you."

I wasn't quite sure how to answer that. "Well, thank you," I said.

"I prayed for a strong woman who had faith, who was as pretty on the inside as the outside, and who wanted to experience all life has to offer."

"God does answer prayers."

"No," he said gently. "You don't understand. I prayed for you for three years."

His words reached deep into my heart. "Aren't you glad you waited?"

At the end of the evening, he asked if I would go out with him the next night for New Year's Eve. "If you're not doing anything tomorrow night, I'd really like to spend more time with you."

"I'd like that very much," I answered. I was supposed to meet someone from online in the afternoon, but I'd already decided that I was going to cancel that meeting and not reschedule. In fact, I returned to that site only one more time to close my account.

The next day, New Year's Eve day, we talked and texted all day and finally decided to go out that evening, listen to music, get drinks and something eat, and then see how the night developed. It was a bitterly cold evening, but we had a lot of fun talking and laughing. About 10:30, we decided to get away from the noise and go to his house.

"Do you play ping pong or pool? I have both in my basement," he said.

"I haven't played in years." I don't know how I'd forgotten that I had just played three rounds of pool with one of my cousins when I was in Illinois; I didn't do very well, so maybe that's why I didn't think about it. We played a couple of games of ping pong first and then switched to pool.

"I guess you can play pool," Jerry commented after I sank three balls in a row. That was the night I learned that he was competitive, and I could give him a run for his money. More importantly, it all felt very comfortable.

We popped a bottle of champagne he found in the refrigerator and watched the ball drop on television. We talked and laughed as the new year began, and reluctantly, he took me home. It had been years since I had been up beyond midnight on New Year's Eve, but I was actually giddy about beginning the new year and my birthday month.

Remember how I said I hadn't really enjoyed celebrating my birthday in past years? With all that I had been through, all the work I had done to find my real self that year, I'd decided to celebrate not only my actual birthday but every day during my birthday month. Ringing in the New Year with a really nice guy who was fun to be with certainly fit the bill!

At about noon on New Year's Day, Jerry and I started texting again. We both said what an amazing seventy-two hours it had been since we'd met. We decided to go to the movies that afternoon.

As luck would have it, we ran into a mutual acquaintance and his wife coming out of the theatre. We all exchanged friendly greetings. As the acquaintance hugged me, he whispered in my ear, "Do you know what you're doing?"

I replied, "I think I can handle it. Thanks."

We engaged in small talk for a couple of minutes and then said goodbye. As we walked into the theatre, Jerry asked, "Are you okay with this? Going public, I mean?"

I grinned. "Sure. You do know it will be all over Newtown by Wednesday, right?"

"Yes." And that was that. We were a couple.

It was back to the reality of the real world on Tuesday morning. Of course, the day began with Jerry and me texting each other. As I drove to work that morning, I had a call with my personal banker.

You may remember that Bill has been a good friend over the years, so our conversations were always part business, part personal. After we concluded our business discussion, I asked, "Bill, why didn't you ever introduce me to Jerry Agasar before?"

"I don't know. Why do you ask?"

"We went on a blind date Friday night, and we've seen each other every day since."

"Oh my gosh, when's the wedding! You're both so energetic," Bill said. "I can see you two together doing great things."

"Whoa, slow down there," I said. "We're just dating right now."

He chuckled. "I know, but I'm ready to put that wedding on the calendar when you do."

I wasn't ready for any wedding yet. Meanwhile, though, it was still my January birthday month, and I was going to enjoy it. Over the next days, I continued with my plans to celebrate in both big and small ways throughout the month. I got together with friends I hadn't seen for a while and had long phone conversations with others who were too far away to see in person. I went to breakfasts and lunches, dinner, and dancing. I listened to music, read, and went shopping just so I could walk around and see what was new. I even planned a party at the end of the month. Not for my birthday, really, just to celebrate life.

As I was still working on me, I opened up and began telling people about my self-care journey. I was completely taken aback when several people told me I'd inspired them to take a look at their own wellness. What I heard humbled and amazed me. I had also been posting on social media, and the comments of encouragement I got in response were overwhelming. I did not think things could get much better than they were. I was happy and living, really living!

At the same time, Jerry and I spent more time getting to know each other. We probably had more quality time in those first days together than most couples do in several months. On day six after our blind date, he came to my house for dinner and met my youngest son. On the next day, he met my friend Kathy, who had been part of my support team as her husband used to watch my kids before and after school. She let him know right up front that he had best not hurt me because there would be hell to pay if he did. He rolled with that like a champ. Then, a couple of days later, I met two of his kids— all that within ten days of our first meeting each other.

Day eleven was a Monday, a long day for both of us. True to his word, Jerry called me at the end of his day while doing his notes. "Hey Cath, how are you?"

I was sitting on the couch with my feet curled under me. "I'm okay," I said. Actually, though, I wasn't. I was in a bit of a spiral and trying to not be.

He heard something in my voice right away. "You don't sound okay. What's the matter?"

I took a deep breath and let it out. "I just had a phone call from Bryan." It still felt a little strange to talk about my older son's situation with someone I'd met so recently, but it also felt right. "It kind of upset me," I said. "Sometimes, he gets pretty manipulative, and I end up feeling bad."

At that point, Bryan was still serving a jail sentence. When he and I spoke, he sometimes tried to play on my guilt, or suggest that I could help him more if I really chose to. I knew that I'd had to let him make his own choices and deal with the consequences himself. As a parent, though, I often still found that very hard to accept.

Jerry asked me a little more about the conversation, and I told him more about my feelings. Then he said, "Do you want me to come over?"

I didn't want him to put himself out for me. "You don't have to," I said. "I know you've had a long day. I'll be all right."

"No, I think you need some support. I'll be done with my notes in a few minutes, and then I'll be over."

"Only if you want to," I said. At the same time, I couldn't help thinking he was right: I did need support.

About half an hour later, he arrived at my house. He came into the front hall, took off his coat, and put his arms around me. It was so nice to have human contact and understanding. He didn't judge, or condemn, or offer unsolicited advice: he just offered me comfort.

We sat in the living room talking for a while, talking about Bryan. Then, without any prompting, Jerry asked, "When do you next visit him?"

Why do you ask? "I don't know, but I'll find out," I said.

"Would you like me to go with you?"

I couldn't quite believe it. I'd known he was kind, but this went above and beyond. "You would do that for me?"

He smiled. "Of course. I care about you, and I want you to know you're not alone. I also want Bryan to know that I'm in your life now."

At that moment, all I could answer was, "Thank you." This guy had only known me for eleven days, but he was willing to go with me to visit my son in jail. I couldn't express what that meant to me or what *he* was beginning to mean to me as an encourager, comforter, and supporter.

We talked the next evening again. Toward the end of our chat, Jerry said, "You know, I think I'm falling in love with you."

I laughed. It felt perfectly easy and natural to say, "That's good to know because I've already fallen."

Jerry was a little taken aback. "How do you know so quickly?"

I understood that he still had emotional baggage from the past that he needed to deal with, and that this was his way of telling me he needed time. That was fine. It didn't change the way I felt, but I didn't feel impatient, either, or anxious for him to hurry up and devote himself to me. Things would unfold as they were supposed to. By this time, I knew beyond a shadow of a doubt that we were together by divine design. The next morning I gave him a card, in which I wrote, "Stop looking back, I'm right beside you." I think that card was as much for me as it was for him. I didn't need a man in my life to complete me, but I had a lot to offer someone in my life.

Expressing my feelings helped me take the next step in opening my life and my heart again.

~

The next Saturday, Jerry asked me to help him host a football playoff party at his house. It was to celebrate the Philadelphia Eagles' first playoff game for 2018. (If you're keeping track, we were now just two weeks into our relationship.) I like sports, but I hadn't paid attention to professional sports for quite some time. Plus, I didn't own a single piece of Eagles gear, so I had to fix that before the party.

Jerry had told me that he'd invited the staff from his office to come over and watch the game. I had met a few of them, and they were nice people, so I thought 'okay, this should be fun.' However, when I arrived at his house that Saturday in my brand-new Eagles gear to start getting food together, I realized that Jerry had invited more than just his staff. His father and his brothers were there, and some of his friends too. The house was filled with people.

I was a little startled, but everything went pretty smoothly. After the game, we were mingling and laughing as one by one, people began to leave. I found his brothers easy to talk with, and his dad was charming. In fact, as he hugged me goodbye, Jerry's dad said, "Welcome to the family, dear. We'll see you soon."

My birthday was five days later. Jerry made a big deal about taking me to dinner after his shift the night before. Since I lived to the south and we were going to dinner to the north, he asked if I could get to his office so we could leave from there. I arrived at the appointed time. After he greeted me with a hug and kiss, he asked, "Where's your bag?"

"What are you talking about?" I said. "My purse is right here."

He looked confused. "Your bag," he said, "with whatever you need for tonight and tomorrow."

I still didn't understand. "Tonight and tomorrow? You only told me we were going to dinner tonight."

His face went white as he realized he'd forgotten to tell me a key detail about his birthday plan for me. "I can't believe I didn't tell you to pack a bag. Awkward!" Then he started babbling because his shift had gone over, and he was afraid we wouldn't make our dinner reservation.

I interrupted. "If you don't mind, I'll take your car and run home for a few things. I'll meet you back here. That way, you can finish your notes, and we can still make it to dinner."

"I'm so sorry." He looked as anxious as a schoolboy taking his date to the prom. "Are you sure you don't mind? I'm really embarrassed."

I didn't mind at all. The "old me" might have felt panicked at the sudden change in plans, but the new me was ready for adventure. "No, I'm looking forward to dinner. I'll be back as quick as I can."

I got back in less than an hour. Jerry and I had a wonderful dinner, with Brussels sprouts, of course, and checked into a B&B on the canal in New Hope, Pennsylvania, as beautiful snow started falling. The world was just on the outskirts of reality; the world consisted of just us. What a wonderful way to move into my birthday!

On the day of my birthday, we walked along the canal. Rather than wear my coat, I put on an extra snow jacket Jerry had brought. I have to tell you that it stung just a bit to wear it—a Penn State jacket on an Illinois girl, after all—but we had so much fun in the snow that I was soon smiling and joking that it must be love to be so happy in the jacket! Although the entire day was a gift, I opened a card at breakfast with salsa dance lessons starting in two weeks. Then, that evening, Jerry gave me another card with tickets to the James Taylor/ Eagles concert coming up that summer. *Wow*, I thought. *I guess we're going to be together for a while.*

The following week, we donned our Eagles gear again (I had two Eagles shirts by then). Just before the game, though, we went to visit my oldest son.

I still couldn't believe Jerry was willing to go visit Bryan in jail with me, yet that is exactly how the two of them met. And the amazing thing was, the meeting was perfectly comfortable and friendly.

I didn't realize it at the time, but this step was a big one on my journey. Given that I'd had so many issues with Bryan over the years, and there had been so much hurt along the way on both sides of the relationship, I needed to know that anyone I brought into my life would accept Bryan and not judge either my son or me. (This was a big reason why I didn't date for so many years. I knew it wasn't fair to bring a new person into that kind of turmoil, and have the parent/child dynamic affect the new relationship.) That day, my heart filled with awe and hope as I experienced a whole new side of what my relationship with Bryan could be, and what it could mean to have a man in my life as well.

My self-care practices were pretty on track at this point, and I was loving life to the fullest on all fronts, except my house. The following weekend was the last Saturday of the month, the day I'd chosen to have my new life celebration. During that gathering, several people asked why my house had not yet sold. I laughed and said, "I don't know," but even as I said it, I too wondered why it hadn't sold yet.

I lived in an area where houses historically sold almost as soon as they went up on the market. My house had been renovated and was beautifully appointed throughout, so when a friend who was an agent asked me the same question as she said goodbye, I asked her to meet with me so we could talk the next week. I felt that I needed to get this house sold before I could move on to my next chapter. The longer the house stayed on the market, the longer I would have to wait to do that.

Meanwhile, I had to admit that as much as I enjoyed my life on all fronts at that point, house hunting was turning out to be neither fun nor fruitful. I prayed about finding a place with energy and life. Every weekend, I went out to look at possible places, but nothing seemed quite right.

The night after my life celebration party, as Jerry was getting ready to leave my house, he asked, "Are you going to buy a new place and then rent it out?"

For a minute, I didn't know what he meant. "What?" I asked.

He looked me in the eye. "You know where this is going."

Was he saying what I thought he was saying? Too much to think about at that moment. I shook my head and told Jerry, "We'll need to talk about this."

Because I was truly working on myself, I decided that I needed to stay focused on what was important and trust that God would take care of all the worries. House hunting and selling went on the back burner, so to speak, and I came back to celebrating the little things in my life. I felt truly blessed. Each day, I saw life in new ways.

Right after my birthday, I realized that I was on track to reach my goal of being down forty pounds by the end of January, so I decided to get another tattoo to celebrate. I set up an appointment, selected the elements I wanted in the design, and gave them to the artist to complete the final version. She did a beautiful job of combining the Celtic symbol for strength intertwined with a rose for beauty. The design celebrated my new beginnings, my new life and strength, and beauty, daily reminders of just how far I have come on this journey to wellness and self-care.

Jerry and I met for a light meal after I got my second tattoo. While we were talking, he brought up house hunting again. "Are you going to look at houses tomorrow?"

"I am. Five places, I think."

"Have you decided what you're going to do yet?"

"I told you, we'll need to talk about this." I smiled. "All I can say right now is I'm not moving twice."

You should have seen his face! It was a mixture of surprise and pleasure. "Okay," he said. "I guess we do need to talk about this."

We actually had many great conversations about our future. They all felt natural and easy as if we'd known each other for years.

During each one, we talked about facts, and our thoughts and feelings, and we asked each other questions and listened attentively to one another.

Two days after my second tattoo, we were in his kitchen preparing food for the Super Bowl. Jerry asked, "Why do you want to be with me? You don't even know me."

I kept stirring whatever I had on the stove but looked around to smile at him. "I know everything I need to know. What I don't know, I'll spend the next fifty-plus years getting to know."

"Wow," he said. "I think I love you!"

As we watched the game, the Eagles made an amazing play, and I commented on it as though we had been talking sports together for years. Jerry grinned. "You really do know the game, don't you?"

"I tried to tell you," I said.

He turned to a friend who was sitting on the other end of the couch. "I'm gonna marry this girl!" he announced.

The following weekend, just thirty-seven days after our blind date, my daughter came home for the weekend and wanted to meet the man I was spending so much time with. Jerry and I decided to have dinner with all of our kids. Five of the six were able to get together that night.

Neither of us had ever envisioned a blended family, but when we saw our kids together that first time, we wondered why it had ever been a concern. They got along famously after the first thirty seconds of awkwardness. We shared childhood stories, laughed, played pool and listened to music, and generally had a lot of fun.

Before dinner, Jerry took me aside and kissed me. "If I'd have known they would get along so well," he said, "I would have proposed to you tonight."

"Well, you still can," I reminded him. I had never thought about getting married again, but I somehow knew everything was happening just as it was supposed to. It was all by divine design.

While he didn't propose that night, the following weekend (Presidents' Day weekend), we went to Cape May, Sea Isle City, and North Wildwood, and began talking earnestly about getting married. By the end of the weekend, we had decided we would marry, as neither of us believed in simply living together. We began to plan and figure out the details. We had known each other just seven weeks and would marry eight weeks later. Crazy, but we knew it was right in every way possible. Within a few short days, we had a guest list, the church, and a place for a family dinner reception. We had ordered invitations and called the family to save the date.

Meanwhile, I fired the first real estate agent who'd been working to sell my house and hired a new one. The new agent came in with full control to make whatever changes needed to be made to sell the house as quickly as possible at the list price. It was taken off the market, minor updates were made, and I earnestly began the down-sizing and packing process. I found a beautiful dress for the wedding and began packing for a cruise that had been planned for more than a year. Needless to say, those two weeks were a whirlwind of activity on many fronts, but not once did I lose sight of my self-care prac-tices. That was truly amazing, and I still marvel at how my self-care practices simply fit into everything I was doing; they were just part of who I was. I was also very confident in my decision to say "yes" to Jerry, which I think made things easy, as though they were supposed to be that way. I remember he asked me one day, "What if people say we're moving too fast?"

I simply replied, "Just tell them I'm pregnant!"

We still laugh about that today...having a baby when we already have six kids between us!

Life has a way of supporting you and letting you know when you need to slow down. My long-awaited cruise was with my friend Sharon; we had so much we wanted to do and see. As fate would have it, I sprained my ankle the very first morning as I got off the treadmill following my workout, and I wound up on crutches for the duration of the cruise. I hobbled around the ship and on our excursions but still had a fabulous time with my friend. That whole week, I was mindful of my self-care in terms of my mind and food and spirit, and physically to the extent I could be, yet I felt a shift inside me that I could not explain. In the past, this would have been something I would have pushed aside and not thought twice about, but given my new desire to live my best life, I did ponder the feeling one afternoon while we were at sea.

As I thought about what I was feeling, I began talking with Sharon. Suddenly, she told me she was angry with me for getting hurt.

I was stunned! It was an accident, as I reminded her. With tears in her eyes, she said, "I know. I was just really looking forward to this time together because things are going to change between us."

That was a wake-up call for me. I hadn't even thought about the changes that might happen in my existing relationships now that I was getting married. How could I have been so short-sighted?

Sharon and I talked about everything for quite some time, during which she assured me she was really happy for me and would still be part of my life. (She also told me she would give me time to settle into my marriage, but she would fully expect me to travel with her again in a few years, "just us girls," she said.)

That was another step on my self-care journey, learning how to adjust so that Sharon and I each continued to feel supported and valued in our friendship, even as life brought changes. It wasn't easy to make these adjustments, but then what is when it is important to us? I knew I would have to be very conscious of and make intentional efforts to maintain and encourage each one of the relationships that meant so much to me. Here I'd thought that the cruise was supposed to just be about having fun and getting away from the cold for a week. God knew better and had a purpose, a plan for me to learn yet another lesson on my self-care journey.

~

During that same cruise, my house went back on the market. Shortly after I sprained my ankle, I received a text from my agent telling me we'd gotten an offer. We countered two days later, and two days after that, we had an agreement. I signed to sell when I returned to Miami. Within a week, my house had sold for the full asking price.

I was elated, and a little shocked that fear hadn't set in. Again, looking back, I can now see that it was because of the self-care practices I had been following, all the emotional work I had been doing on myself, that I was not panicked or worried. I was ready to move forward.

If you've ever packed up a house in which you have lived for more than a few years, you understand the stress of packing and discarding. It can be extremely grueling. I spent the next two weeks cleaning, packing, donating, and pitching all over the house. There were inspections, minor items that had to be addressed for the sale to be completed, and furniture to move or sell. On top of all that, I had to merge two households into one so that Jerry and I would both be comfortable in his house. Thank goodness for Kelsey, my organizer, and packer extraordinaire! She truly was a godsend and kept me sane throughout the entire process. She brought a level of detachment to the process, helping me to not get sentimental over things and staying focused on the end goal.

I moved houses three weeks before my second wedding. The day after a big snowstorm, I looked out the front window in what would be my new house to see a cardinal sitting on a branch right outside the window looking right at me. The timing was strangely perfect, because two nights before, I'd had another dream about my late husband. He'd simply been standing and smiling at me, and then he faded away. They say that when a cardinal comes to visit you, it's a loved one who has gone to heaven, coming back to say that everything will be okay. I took that as my final confirmation that my new life was before me and could be all I wanted it to be.

That turned out to be a very good thing. On the weekend that my furniture went from one house to another, Jerry had made lunch plans for us. I thought it was with some friends, but when we got to the restaurant and were escorted to the table, there sat all six of our children. He had arranged for everyone to be there.

He told me, "I wanted them to be here because these last twelve weeks have been incredible. You have brought me incredible joy, and with them as witnesses, and with their approval, I would love to encourage you, support you, and love you for the rest of my life. Will you marry me?"

Of course, there was only one answer. "Yes!" I said.

He got down on one knee and put a ring on my finger. I cried, and the kids clapped. One even asked Jerry if he'd been worried about my answer, and everyone laughed. Family has always been very important to me. It was extremely special to have all of our children present at that moment.

Yes, fifteen weeks after a blind date, my two grown sons walked me down the aisle at my church. I married the man who had become part of my heart in a very short amount of time; a man who loved me as much as I loved him, and would never take me for granted.

That day, Jerry and I promised to love, honor, and support each other in every way. Also, although we didn't speak a vow to this effect, we promised to love each other's children as though they were our own. It mattered to us that all of our children were part of that day and our marriage; it mattered that our first family photo was of all eight of us together at the church. It did not matter that it was Friday the 13th. It only mattered that we were together.

Epilogue

For you shall go out in joy and be led forth in peace;
the mountains and the hills before you shall
break forth in singing, and all the trees
of the field shall clap their hands.
Isaiah 55:12

That would be a nice way to end the telling of my story, but in truth, my journey to self-care continued beyond that happy day. While I understood the principles behind self-care, I learned more about me and my relationship with my self-care practices during the weeks following the wedding.

Jerry and I had so much to do in the house, so much unpacking and purging and settling in as a new couple. I still had a business to run, as did he, and clients to see and care for. We each had three more children to care about and love; yes, they were all grown, but those new relationships took new commitment. And we needed to tend the relationships we'd already had, which were changing now that we'd started our new life together. And on top of all this, we had the newness of our marriage, negotiating routines and rhythms, nurturing and managing our daily lives.

It was a lot of "stuff" all at once. Some days, the waters got murky. I kept self-care in my schedule, but sometimes it stopped being a priority. During those first few months after the wedding, if I got exercise three or four days a week, I was happy.

I still felt good, kept my weight down, and added in new adventures of biking and hiking with my husband. We traveled and visited family, managing what seemed like a pretty active life for newlyweds, and I loved every minute of it. We traveled to Salt Lake City for my nephew's graduation three weeks after the weeding and then to England and France for a honeymoon in the fall; attended weddings of friends and family members; traveled to Las Vegas and Atlanta on business; and prepared to have the entire family home for Thanksgiving.

We had a wonderful time with all of our kids at home, and we both felt as though we had come full circle. I loved it so much that I wanted to capture the feeling of family we'd experienced and hold it for eternity. But just thirty short hours later, I was hit with another challenge that rocked my new world: my oldest son called me, asking me to bail him out, yet again.

I saw, then, that I hadn't internalized my self-care practices fully enough yet. In my worry for my son, I went back into the dark places I'd been in years earlier, and my fear began to rise. This time, though, I didn't have to face it or make decisions all alone. I had someone beside me who would help me stay strong and do what I needed to do without judgment. I also had family surrounding me. The fresh challenge set me back, but ultimately, it also gave me hope.

Although my heart broke for my son, I knew—again— that I had to let him deal with the consequences of his actions. At this point, though, I unintentionally let my emotional eating habits creep back into my life; this meant I ate processed snacks and foods that included refined sugars. By Christmas Eve, I still ate veggies, but I also snacked on the numerous cookies and treats patients had given my husband for the holidays. I made appetizers with caramel dip and apples but ate more caramel dip than apple. By the time we rolled into January, I needed a self-care reboot.

And there it is. Self-care is not about being so regimented that we forget to live life. It is not about starving or staying away from foods that we enjoy. It is not about denying ourselves in any way. It is about taking care of what your body needs when it needs it and paying attention to moderation rather than excesses. From time to time, every self-care journey will need a reboot, not a kick in the pants because you messed up. Life is for living. Just remember what you're living for.

So here I am, almost thirty-one months after truly starting my journey to self-care, and I am beginning again with a reboot. I'm not starting over, but I am picking up where I left off. I remember how good it felt to take care of me, and I'm adjusting my routines so I can get back to where I want to be. Will my self-care routine be exactly what it was before I got married? Probably not, but I'm sure it will have many of those elements and practices, and it will definitely be all about me living life to the fullest.

I have no idea where my story will go from here, except that I know it will continue to go forward: that's why it's called a journey. Just like you, I have only one life to live, but each day I have a new chance to make a difference in my world. I get to choose how I will live. I get to choose how I will show up each day, and best of all, I get to choose how I love myself and those I choose to have in my life. So today, I choose to continue my self-care journey. I choose to live my best life every day!

Acknowledgments

When it comes to raising children or planning successful events or doing mission work, I have often heard it said, "it takes a village." Writing this book falls into the category of "it takes a village," so I need to take a moment to offer my heartfelt thanks to the village that helped me get this work published.

First and foremost, I thank God for the abilities He has given me, and for the journey He has been on with me. I have learned more than I ever thought possible, and I have a feeling there is still more to learn in my future, so I am simply grateful beyond measure.

To Jerry, my husband, my partner, my best friend, my encourager, my supporter, my constant accountability, and voice of reason: you are by far the BEST gift I have ever received. If this is what a year and a half together looks like, I can only imagine the places we will go and the things we will do going forward. Thank you for complementing me and loving me so completely. I absolutely love US!

To my children, Jennifer, Bryan, and Andrew Jacob, I love you all! You have lived through some dark times with me, taught me valuable lessons, laughed with me, cried with me, and through it all still love me! To my son-in-law, Dustin, thank you for joining our family, accepting us and loving our "Miss J." To my children, Andrew Gerald, Alexandra, and Michael, thank you for accepting me into your lives and giving me three more children to love and cherish. I never thought I would have six children, but now that I do, I think it is awesome, and so are each of you! I do not know where the journey will take us, but we will do it as a family.

To my parents, Ronnie and Sue, for always loving and encouraging me to live my best life. You are both my heroes, and I could not have asked for better role models. God sure knew what he was doing when he made us family; I could not have chosen better if I had to. I love you both!

To my sisters and brothers, Chris, Rich, Alicia, Joe, Kathy, and Tim: you may not be blood, but God made you family. Your continuous love, prayers, and support over the years mean more to me than words can express. You have cried, laughed, and celebrated with me. You have always made me feel welcomed, loved, and accepted, and I thank you from the bottom of my heart for allowing me to choose you and choosing me in return. Life has taken us a little further apart these days, but know that you are never far from my heart.

To my forever sisters and care team, Beverley, Gail Marie, Tiffany, Sharon, and Suzanne: you are each amazing women of faith, love, and compassion in your own right, but together...wow! You never pulled any punches, but you held me accountable and made me see—really see—myself. You encouraged me to keep going when I wanted to give up, and you loved me when I did not think I deserved it. You traveled with me, laughed with me, have taken my phone calls in the middle of the night, cried with me, and sat in silence when there was nothing more to say. Thank you for helping me see there was a journey to be taken.

To Shari-Beth for helping me to realize that nothing was going to change until I got started, and for helping me to embrace the motto, "bring it on!"

To Ian and Lynne: you came into my life as colleagues but quickly became family. I will always be grateful for the way you listen, care, encourage, and laugh with me, and the ease with which we share our lives across the pond.

To my team, Jessica, Nicole, Christine, Doreen, Tonia, Leslie,

Ashley, Alyssa, and Carla and all my clients and associates: you have each shared a little part of your lives with me and through that sharing encouraged me to see more than just what is in front of me. Thank you for inspiring me to learn and grow to make the spa a better place for wholistic living and education. You each shine and bring a smile to my face.

To my book team, Debby and Kathie: you get me! You are each extremely talented, and I love working with you. Thanks for encouraging me, listening to my stories, keeping me focused, and helping me create a work that I am really proud of. You both rock!

And finally, to you, the reader, for honoring me by reading this book, for, in your reading, I can share a piece of myself and fulfill a small part of my bigger purpose. Thank you for allowing me into your life to share my story; I pray you will be blessed as you read the pages and find your journey to self care.

Be well...
Cathy

About the Author

Cathy Agasar believes that there were incredible gifts that came after the sudden death of her first husband. Using that experience as a catalyst for personal growth, Cathy completely transformed her life. She lives with her beloved husband, Jerry, and their family in Bucks County, PA. This is her first book. For more information, visit www.agasarfamilywellcare.com.

CPSIA information can be obtained
at www.ICGtesting.com
Printed in the USA
LVHW021457110520
655010LV00007B/334